THE ART OF HERALDRY

———— ✳ ————

The Art of Heraldry

CARL-ALEXANDER von VOLBORTH

TIGER BOOKS INTERNATIONAL

LONDON

First published in the UK 1987 by Blandford Press,
a Cassell imprint

Copyright © 1987 Carl-Alexander von Volborth

This edition published in 1991 by
Tiger Books International, London

ISBN 1-85501-154-9

Typeset by August Filmsetting, Haydock, St Helens

Printed in Hong Kong by
South China Printing Co (1988) Ltd

*To Diana, my wife, in gratitude for her
assistance and enthusiasm, for her suggestions
and constant readiness for discussion of ideas.*

CONTENTS
———— ✽ ————

PART III
AN INTERNATIONAL EXHIBITION OF HERALDIC WORKS
BY ARTISTS & ARTISANS FROM THE END OF THE NINETEENTH
CENTURY TILL TODAY

FOREWORD

———— ✳ ————

THE AIM OF this book is to draw more attention to the artistic side of heraldry, which in my opinion has been pretty much ignored by contemporary literature. It is meant to be a picture book of contrasts, exhibiting a great variety of heraldic art and craft from the past and the present, and is intended to contribute to a growing general awareness of the artistic possibilities of heraldry. It is also directed to anybody who might have to deal with heraldic art in the course of his work or likes to try his talents as an amateur.

Part I is intended as a technical guide for the student, offering some basic findings and suggestions on how to go about the designing of a coat of arms. Some of these may strike the experienced artist as perhaps too rigid or subjective, yet as crutches for the beginner they can be quite useful.

How heraldic art and craft have been influenced by various historical styles over the centuries is illustrated in **Part II** of the book. These pictures are not always examples of heraldry at its best, but also of quite average work, yet characteristic of its period and geographical environment. Some illustrations, especially from the sixteenth century on, were also chosen because they demonstrate the slow decline of the art until it reached its lowest level around 1800. This does not mean, however, that at the same time more acceptable heraldry had disappeared completely.

History of art gives an account of the noteworthy happenings affecting the field of art, of which heraldry is only a very small section. Yet the development of armorial design cannot be fully appreciated and understood if it is taken out of context, without consideration of the changes that took place in architecture, painting and sculpture from the twelfth century on to at least the beginning of the nineteenth century. For that reason it is suggested that the serious student, who wants to get more closely acquainted with these developments, should also read about this period and in particular its architecture and fine arts. Two very useful works

are Helen Gardner's *Art Through the Ages* and E.H. Gombrich's *The Story of Art*.

There is an incredible wealth of armorial art to be found in most European countries, which seems to have been grossly neglected so far also by the art-historian. It would take a lot of team work and financial effort just to find, collect and pool the pictorial material, not to mention the necessary historical research, to be able one day to present a general survey of the heraldic art treasures of Europe to the public. The author hopes that his meagre attempt to make a beginning in this direction may inspire others to turn their attention to this artistically and historically interesting field.

Part III should be looked upon as an exhibition of heraldic work, created within the past hundred years, which may also to a certain extent convey an impression of the status quo of heraldic art. Some of the artists whose works are reproduced are deceased, others are young, middle-aged or older. Some readers will perhaps ask why certain names known to them are not represented. In the first place, I might not have been aware of their existence. Secondly, not every artist I approached answered favourably or at all to my request to join the show, while others (or their heirs or publishers) would have participated, but under conditions which were impossible for me to accept.

Ample knowledge of heraldry and its rules and customs in the various countries of Europe can be very useful to the artist, especially if he lives in the United States, Canada, Australia or wherever people of different ethnic backrounds make up the population. Since *The Art of Heraldry* was originally planned as a supplementary part of *Heraldry: Customs, Rules and Styles* (Blandford Press 1981), the study of this earlier manual is naturally recommended to the beginner to attain the necessary basic understanding of the regulating principles and the spirit of this international subject.

Carl-Alexander von Volborth Antwerp, 1985.

PART I
*
HERALDIC DESIGN
*

INTRODUCTION

———— * ————

WHEN IN THE first third of the twelfth century knights began to have their shields and other equipment decorated with simple marks of identification, they would never have believed that not much later this procedure would cause a new form of art and a new science to be born. If they had been told, they might have reacted as we would if somebody predicted that our present traffic signs would have a similar future. And yet, the simple devices painted on the shield, the combination of their tinctures of colour and metal, as well as the shapes of the shields and the crested helms with their mantling, soon became an artistic challenge.

Seeing is a biological but also a spiritual process, which might perhaps explain why the majority of people seem to have difficulties in recognizing artistic beauty because they disapprove of or dislike the subject matter. At any rate, they seem to need an easily recognizable illustration of something they know already, and they feel lost if the aesthetic aspects of a work of art are predominant. In other words, a design is not beautiful or repulsive because of its underlying theme. The arrangements of colours, tonal values, lines, shapes, and sometimes also texture, determine its artistic appeal. If two artists are given the same assignment, their different approach to the problem would result in two different works of art. In spite of the fact that in both cases the subject is the same, we might according to our taste and understanding prefer one to the other.

Beauty is something that may appeal without being necessarily understood. But we all feel slightly different about beauty, depending on our personality and background. There is no objective criterion. *De gustibus non est disputandum.*

Even a realistic painting is an abstraction from natural objects, as far as life, size, dimensions and light are concerned, and the feeling of perspective or deep space on a flat surface is created by optical illusion. The pigments of the paint box cannot compete at all with the intensity and brightness of natural light. The artist's possibilities are limited by

his range of tonal values, which reach only from black to white. Take a picture with brilliant colours and strong light and dark contrasts into a dark room and the optical illusion does not work any more.

Heraldic art forces the artist to work within even stronger limitations, since his main subject is the coat of arms, which is itself subject to strict rules that have to be respected. There is, however, enough freedom left for an individual pictorial interpretation, which has saved heraldry from becoming sterile and, to a certain extent, made it possible to adjust itself to the different styles of history of art without losing too much of its basic character.

There is much more to an heraldic design than simply to assemble its different parts and tincture them in the prescribed way. After all, we not only want an heraldically correct but also an aesthetically appealing picture.

The design should be a compact unit, a cohesive composition, a union of all the parts involved. The arrangement of lines, shapes, colours and tonal values should be such that our eyes are led all over the picture without wanting to leave it. The balance of the entire pattern should be carefully kept, be it in a formal or informal way.

Of a single coat of arms a great variety of designs is possible, depending on the artist's personal range and style. But in spite of the fact that he may feel forced in some cases to use ruler and compasses, he should try to avoid making a coat of arms look like a geometric assignment. In projecting the composition the first thought should be given to dynamic qualities. Movement and tension are gained by counter-balancing and contrasting items. Balance, if handled formally, might lend a certain feeling of dignity to the design, but it could just as well create a monotonous effect.

The artist should work on a graded scale of attraction. He must try to bring all the components into the right proportion, which means that he has to determine the size of the proper share of an element of design in relation to the share of others in order to achieve the desired effect. The rhythm of pattern and lines is greatly responsible for the final outcome.

In this connection it must be mentioned that there is quite a difference between a design in colour and a simple line drawing. The quality of the line drawing depends exclusively on an overall pattern, created by the swing and rhythm of lines. Such a pattern, if filled in with colours, may not have the same appeal any more, since the distribution of the prescribed tinctures might destroy the harmonious effect or upset the balance. Thus, when working on a design supposed to be in colour, one must try to bring a linear pattern in accord with a pattern of colours and tonal values. The artist must at all times be aware of all the inter-related elements of his work.

The designer of new armorial bearings should try to arrange the charges and tinctures in such a way that even an inferior artistic interpretation could not destroy the basic beauty of such arms. In other words: it is much easier to produce an appealing picture of an originally well-designed coat of arms than to make a beauty of something that had not much artistic quality in its original conception.

Colours have qualities well worth considering for anybody working on the draft of a new coat of arms. They can be warm or cool, light or dark, brilliant or dull. In relationship to other colours they can give the impression of advancing or receding. From red to reddish purple they seem to radiate warmth, while from reddish purple to blue they gradually get cooler. Pure black and white represent the strongest contrast. They are the opposite ends of the full range of tonal values and neutral as colours. Green is a colour mix of yellow and blue. Its warmth or coolness depend on which of the two is predominant in the mixture. A yellowish green is much warmer than a blueish one. The warm colours are the ones that seem to come forward, while green stays in the middle, and the cool colours recede.

Colours may also have an emotional effect, having their own character qualities. Yellow can be festive, radiant and gay; orange can be in addition to that majestic and stimulating. In gold, depending on its particular hue, we find about the same qualities. Red is generally looked upon as an exciting colour. Perhaps that is the reason why it is widely used as a danger signal. A red light makes us stop in time. It would appear to be much closer than a green or blue light in the same distance. Red can be stimulating, but also disturbing and irritating. Purple can have moody and soothing, but also subduing and depressive, effects, while blue is cool,

fresh and withdrawn.

Tonal values are of great importance for the overall balance. Draw two circles of equal size on white paper. Fill in one of them with black and you will find that the white sphere seems to be advancing, of lighter optical weight and larger than the black one.

It was quite normal in medieval times for a coat of arms to have one colour and one metal only. This provided enough contrast for the simple devices supposed to be recognized from a greater distance. The colour would be effective through its intensity, the metal through its reflecting the light.

In connection with the display of armorial bearings we should not forget the complementary colours. If we place a coat of arms with predominantly red and white colours against a green background, we get a pleasing and harmonious effect, since red and green are complementary to each

1. *The coat of arms of the author. The subdued and cool greenish-grey background makes the warm red come forward, and as a darker tonal value it causes the white to stand out. (See Fig. 518.)*

2. *The ancient coat of arms of the House of Savoy. Blue and yellow represent a strong colour accord. The background emphasizes harmoniously the yellow of helm, crest and mantling. On a green background the accentuation of the red in the shield would be stronger, while the tincture of the crest would lose some of its appeal, being complementary to a blueish colour. (See Fig. 514.)*

3. *The coat of arms of a member of the German family von Brauchitsch, who is a Knight of St John (Johanniterorden). Black and white, the strongest tonal values, could be placed on any other colour. Here the warm brick red of the background emphasizes the cool silvery grey in the arms.*

other. The red gives the impression of being in front of the green, and the neutral white stands out because it is the lightest tonal value in this composition. If the tinctures were red and yellow, a blue background would also work out, since blue and yellow affect each other in a complementary manner. A red background of a darker or lighter tonal value than that in the arms would emphasize the yellow and weaken the red areas. The safest way, but by no means the only one, is to place an heraldic design of predominantly one colour and one metal against a background of a colour which is complementary to one of the two.

4. *The coat of arms of the Bockhorst family, Braunschweig, West Germany. The motto is: BEDENKEN, HANDELN, BESTEHEN ('Consider, act, persist').*

The design of a new coat of arms must be carefully planned. After all, the designer is responsible for something that is going to be pinned down in the blazon and might be used by a family or a corporation for a long time to come. Unfortunately, not every heraldist responsible for the creation of a new coat of arms could be called an artist.

All over Europe, particularly from the seventeenth to the nineteenth century, innumerable armorial bearings have been granted which make anybody cringe who has a little artistic instinct and heraldic taste. Innumerable ancient arms of nobles, who had been raised to a higher degree of nobility, have been augmented, quartered and embellished in many ways. But these 'improvements' were not always a success and many coats of arms lost their original beauty.

Today most heraldic authorities and heraldists seem to be well aware of the sins of the past, and it is to be hoped that common sense, combined with knowledge, talent and good taste, will help to keep up the comparatively high standards of contemporary heraldic art.

Each of the different line drawings (**Figs. 5–16**) has its own character. If we imagine a knight's head under the helm and the shield on his left arm, he seems to sit (**Fig. 5**) on a horse that could be standing, as it could also be in motion. The reason for this is the short mantling, which does not add much to the expression of the drawing. It does, however, counter-balance the bill of the swan.

In **Fig. 6** the movement of the lines of the much richer mantling is stronger, as if the knight was riding at a gallop.

In **Fig. 7** the flapping of the mantling could create the impression that he is riding at a canter.

The movement of the lines and the pattern it creates are responsible for the final effect of the line-drawing. The head of the swan in **Fig. 5** draws more attention than in **Figs. 6** and **7** because it is the only spot in the drawing in which black lines come that close together. The exceptional always stands out. In **Fig. 6** the strong competition of the mantling destroys that effect. The comparatively dense, curvy-linear handling of the mantling on both sides of the rather plain shield frames the latter and emphasizes its prominence.

Let us assume that the swan's head and neck are white, while the arms are Sable, a chevron argent. As can be seen in **Figs. 8, 9, 10** and **15**, the design becomes bottom-heavy, i.e. our attention is directly drawn to the shield, which is by no means wrong from an heraldic point of view. Seen with the eyes of an artist, however, the crest is much too light in

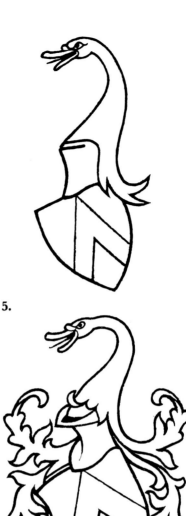

5.

6.

7.

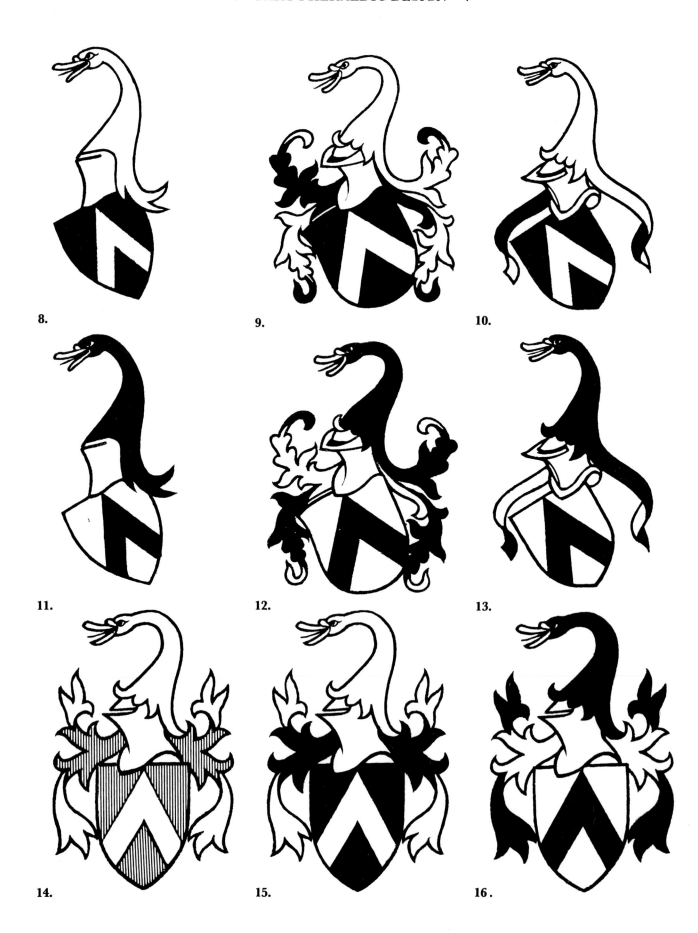

8.

9.

10.

11.

12.

13.

14.

15.

16.

17. *The coat of arms of the ancient von Erlach family, Switzerland. Since the tinctures of a coat of arms are of the utmost importance, they are indicated by hatching. Most heraldists today reject hatching for aesthetic reasons. They feel it could ruin the beauty of a line drawing. This may well be, in many cases, yet on the other hand a coat of arms in line drawing could belong to more than one party, especially if the charges are commonly used and simple, as for instance a cross, a chevron, a lion or an eagle. As long as such a drawing is not accompanied by its description or the name of the armiger, it seems to me better to indicate the tinctures. If this is not done too crudely, it could even add to the body of the drawing.*

optical weight. If the swan had a black bill and a black collar around its neck, the balance of attraction would be restored.

In **Fig. 9** the left part of the mantling seems to be much heavier than the right one, because more than half of it is black. In connection with the main movement of the black pattern this gives an impression as if the design could roll over to the left. In the much simpler mantling of **Fig. 10** the balance is better, since the heavier weight is closer to the centre of the design than the one on the right. In all three cases the balance creating a more compact unit could be achieved by adding smaller charges in the right places, light ones on the shield and dark ones on the crest.

Let us assume that the swan's head and neck were black, while the arms were: Argent, a chevron sable. In **Figs. 11, 12, 13** and **16**, the balance is much better and we get the impression of a cohesive composition. The adding of additional charges could enrich but not necessarily improve the designs.

The unity and compactness of each design could be emphasized by placing it against a background darker than its light parts and lighter than its dark parts.

Figs. 14, 15 and **16** are of the same basic design, but the shields stand upright and the mantling is drawn in formal balance. In spite of the informally-balanced designs of helm and crest, this gives us a feeling of equilibrium and a static quality. The hatching in **Fig. 14** was done to show that a lighter tonal value than black creates a softer contrast to the white, leaving more prominence to the crest than in **Fig. 15**.

TINCTURES

*

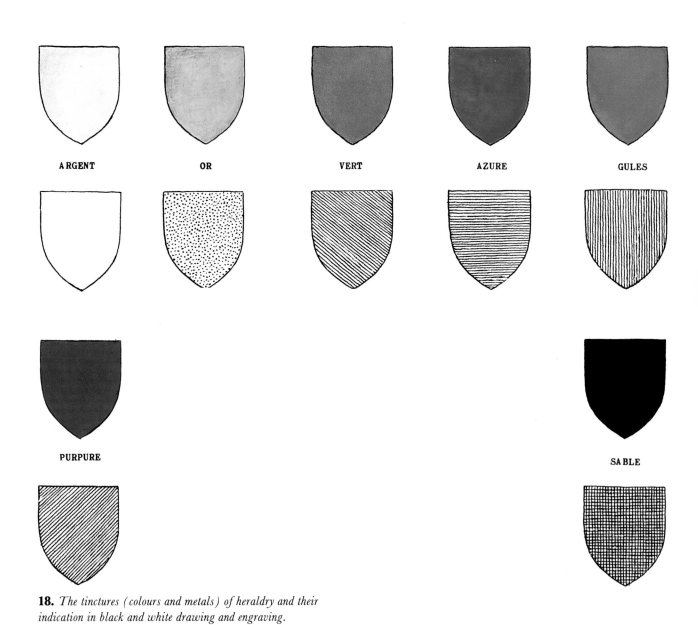

ARGENT   OR   VERT   AZURE   GULES

PURPURE   SABLE

18. *The tinctures (colours and metals) of heraldry and their indication in black and white drawing and engraving.*

19. *The coat of arms of Charles John Burnett, Commander of the Venerable Order of St John, Edinburgh, Scotland. Since the tinctures of face, hands and hair of the angel are not described in the blazon, it must be assumed that they are of natural colour, called proper in heraldry. Strictly speaking, the display of the neckbadge is an anachronism in conjunction with an armorial design based on the style of the fourteenth century. Nevertheless, the rules of the Order prescribe this kind of usage, while in Scottish heraldry a modern style, inspired by the late fourteenth century, is in vogue.*

20. *The coat of arms of Gerard Crotty, Fermoy, Co. Cork, Ireland.*

21. *The coat of arms of the West German general Wolfgang Malecha, Knight of St John (Johanniterorden).*

22. *The original arms of the German Counts von Keller. In engraved work the indication of black is possible only by using a criss-cross pattern.*

HERALDIC COLOURS SHOULD be strong and true. Red, for instance, should neither be too purplish nor too orange, nor lean towards pink or brown. Blue should not be purplish or greenish. Green should not lean too much towards yellow or blue, and the heraldic purpure is more red-purple than blue-purple. Gold may be represented by yellow, preferably a mixture of yellow and ochre. White may substitute for silver, but a watery, very light grey represents the metal more appropriately. It is possible, but not recommendable, to 'tune' the pallette to a key of colours more subtle in effect, as long as the tinctures look right in relation to each other

and are easily recognized for what they ought to be according to the blazon.

An important heraldic rule is that a metal object should not be laid upon a metal field, nor a coloured one upon colour. This rule does not apply to furs or to charges blazoned as proper. Other exceptions are cases in which the field is varied of colour and metal. Here a charge, resting on the field as a whole, may be either of metal or of colour. There are also exceptions as far as bordures are concerned and charges surmounting not only the field but also another charge.

FUR PATTERNS

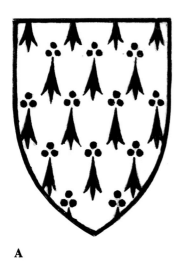

A

B

C

D

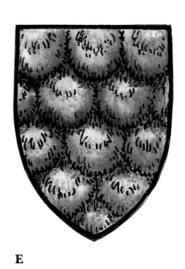

E

F

G   **H**   **I**

23. *The furs of heraldry descend from the real furs which were used in the twelfth and thirteenth centuries (in addition to the tinctures) to embellish the shield. Fur patterns like B, C and D are normally white and blue but other tinctures occur also, in which case they must be stated in the blazon.*

A. *Ermine consists of a pattern of black tails or spots on white. Variations of ermine are ermines, erminois and pean. Ermines is a black field with white spots; erminois has black spots on a gold background and pean gold spots on black.*

B. *The vair patterns have their origin in the fur of the grey squirrel. A number of skins were sewn together, alternating the bluish grey of the back and the white of the belly. Illustration B represents an early form of vair, drawn with wavy lines.*

C. *Counter-vair. If the second and fourth row of blue skins were right side up, this would be called vair in pale.*

D. *Potent is probably another early form of vair. In counter-potent the blue pieces are arranged as in C.*

E. *Natural fur.*

F. *Vairy of Or and gules.*

G. *Gules papelonné argent.*

H. *Vairy of sable, argent, gules and Or.*

I. *Vair en point.*

24. *Ancient and modern versions of ermine-tails.*

THE PROPORTIONS OF
A COAT OF ARMS
———— ✳ ————

25. *The coat of arms of the Fröwler family of Basel, Switzerland, fourteenth century. See Fig. 496.*

26. *The coat of arms of Ralph, Lord Basset of Drayton, K.G. 1368, died 1390.*

27. *The coat of arms of Sir Bermond Armand de Preissac, K.G. 1380, died c.1384.*

28. *The coat of arms of the Landschaden von Steinach, Neckarsteinach, Hesse, West Germany, 1450. (See Fig. 219.)*

PROBABLY THE BEST way for the artist to find the right proportions for the design of a coat of arms, i.e. the height of the shield in relationship to helm and crest, is first to decide on the style in which he would like to execute his work and then to visualize a knight in full armour of that period. Since shields and helms have gone through important changes in form and size during the first centuries of heraldic existence, it should be beneficial for the designer to study not only artistic examples of the past but also to get acquainted with medieval and Renaissance armoury.

The simplest way is to think of the shield as occupying one half of the achievements height, and

29. *The armorial bearings of the Counts von Kotzebue, an adaptation from a nineteenth-century design. The original arms were 'argent, three roses (2,1) azure' and the crest was the same as the one on the helm in the centre but with blue and silver mantling.*

30. *The coat of arms of the German Counts von Brandenstein-Zeppelin.*

helm and crest the other half, or a little more. Naturally, much depends on the kind of crest that is used. Wings or antlers could be drawn much taller than an animal standing on its four feet.

When Paul von Kotzebue, Russian governor general of Poland, was created a count in 1874, his arms were adjusted to his new dignity (see **Fig. 29**). The Russian eagle (issuant) in chief, bearing the initials of Czar Alexander II in a small shield on its breast, was added as augmentation and the shield ensigned with a count's coronet. Two more helms and two supporters, standing on a compartment, as also a motto, completed the design. At first glance nothing seems to be wrong with it, but on closer scrutiny we notice a few undesirable effects. If it is at all necessary to have more than one helm, then why use the same crest twice? Also these helms may have the right size for the supporters, but would be much too small for the man bearing the shield; and they should not float in mid-air. The coronet of a count is of giant-size, while the supporters look much too small in relation to the shield. Finally, the Russian soldier, wearing a uniform from about 1870, is definitely an anachronism in this setting.

This achievement, however, is but one of so many that have been created in a similar style all over Europe from the seventeenth century on. In those days soldiers would wear uniforms, and the knight in shining armour, his shield emblazoned with a heraldic device, his helm adorned with his crest, belonged to times long gone. Armorial bearings had become emblems which people understood as flat designs, executed in painting, engraving or in relief sculpture. It is therefore not surprising that the feeling for the characteristics of medieval heraldry weakened and new customs and rules appeared, enriching this 'flat' heraldry often in a very unheraldic manner.

A much better design is shown in **Fig. 30** of the coat of arms of the German Counts von Brandenstein-Zeppelin, an adaptation from the original letters patent (Kingdom of Württemberg, 1909). The shield is quartered of: 1 and 4 von Zeppelin; 2 the dominion of Hengstfeld; and 3 the dominion of Geisberg. The inescutcheon bears the arms of the ancient von Brandenstein family. The eagles as supporters are derived from the supporters of the coat of arms of Count Ferdinand von Zeppelin (died in 1917), the pioneer of airships, who was the father-in-law of the first Count von Brandenstein-Zeppelin.

A coronet of a count could have been placed between the two helms, but was probably left out for reasons of style.

The whole composition could rest on something stronger than the thin tree branches, but in general the strong and lively design captures the heraldic spirit of this typically German achievement of arms.

31. *The coat of arms of the Hungarian family Marsovszky de Marsófalva, 1430.*

32. *The coat of arms of the ancient County of Tirol. (See Figs. 192 and 194.)*

33. *The coat of arms of the Dutch heraldic artist Karel van den Sigtenhorst.*

34. *Formally-balanced design of the coat of arms of the Duvernoy family (German branch, now also in the USA), originating from the Franche Comté, France, fourteenth century.*

35. *Many coats of arms are designed in formal balance, except for the helm and the crest. The armorial bearings used by the family of Robert Edward Lee, 1807–1870, American Confederate general.*

THE BASIC DESIGN, or as we could call it the abstract skeleton of a work of art, is mainly responsible for its overall effect. The subject's appeal or lack of such can be emphasized or minimized by the designing artist. The rhythm and swing of lines, the distribution of optical weights, the choice of colour combinations and their particular shades, as well as the balance of the entire composition (formal or informal), create in combination with the given subject the finished work's own peculiar expression. That, in addition, is also influenced by the technique employed by the artist. If he is a sculptor, for instance, he might make the texture of the stone or the grain of the wood add an additional touch to his work.

A coat of arms consists of shield and helm with crest and mantling and sometimes of even more appurtenances. But, in the view of an artist, it also consists of lines, shapes, colours and tonal values; it is an optical pattern, depending for its artistic quality very much on a clever proportionate use of these ingredients.

Figs. 32 and **33** show two informally-balanced designs of armorial bearings.

The design of a coat of arms should be thought of as a unit in style. Which one we choose may depend on the type of crest or the charges on the shield. If, for instance, the charges or the crest figure should be tools, weapons or other objects which made their first appearance in the seventeenth century, one should not use helm, mantling and shield of an earlier period. In doubtful cases it is always better to choose a style from a later period than to commit an anachronism. (See **Figs. 36** and **37**.)

The form in which an heraldic achievement is represented should also depend on the environment in which it is to be displayed. It would not be in the best of taste, for instance, to engrave a coat of arms, kept in the style of the fourteenth century, on a Baroque silver tray. On the other hand, however, a stone-carved coat of arms in the Gothic style might very well go with the functional simplicity of a modern building. Much depends here on the discretion of the artist.

In **Figs. 36** and **37**, the first design (left) was made in accordance with the present Scottish style, inspired by the heraldry of the fourteenth century. However, the author's historical conscience rebelled

36 and **37.** *The coat of arms of Major Terrence C. Manuel, Gloucester, Ontario, Canada. His badge as an Officer of the Venerable Order of St John and the Canadian Forces Decoration are suspended from the shield.*

against the combination of a fourteenth-century barrel helm and a cannon as a crest that may have existed in this form at the end of the fifteenth century. Thus, a second design was tried, in which helm, crest, mantling and shield could be from the same period. If modern decorations are displayed in connection with armorial bearings an anachronistic effect is inevitable, but generally accepted.

The designer of a new coat of arms should try to avoid any object as a charge on the shield or as a crest that had not been invented or was completely unknown when heraldically-decorated equipment was actually used in battle and tournament. An airplane, a locomotive or a microscope look rather odd on a medieval helm or in a shield. Modern battleships or factories, even if they are well stylized, do not belong in an heraldic achievement. There is, however, nothing wrong with the invention of new abstract patterns and forms which adapt themselves to the ancient heraldic spirit.

THE SHIELD
OR ESCUTCHEON

———— ✳ ————

THE SHIELD IS the most important and the only indispensable part of a coat of arms. It can be used by itself, without any other heraldic appurtenance. For that reason the artist could try to make it the centre of attraction of his design, which is not easy since helm and crest are strong competitors and often steal the show. By keeping the charges on the shield flat, simple and stylized, by avoiding perspective and photographic realism, the contrast to helm, crest and mantling, being more dense in their pattern and treated in a more realistic manner, can be intensified and thus could add to the optical weight and importance of the shield.

Since the beginning of paper heraldry, and even earlier, an immense number of arms have been created which are so crowded with quarterings or charges that they resemble the pattern of Eastern carpets, rather than the original, easily legible devices on the medieval knight's shield. When the artist is confronted with such overcrowded armorial bearings, he cannot do more than aim at a satisfactory, well-balanced overall design. (See **Figs. 406** and **407**.) In the design of the Washington arms (**Fig. 38**) the prominence of the shield is caused by its simplicity in contrast to helm, mantling and motto, which accentuate the effect by also acting as a frame. The light shield stands out against the darker background, which is kept in a shade of green, complementary to the red in the arms.

The Kennedy arms (**Fig. 39**) are a little more complicated and in addition of two more tinctures. The black and the gold, repeated only in the torse, are in strong contrast to the bordure of ermine and red and draw the attention to the shield.

Fig. 40 shows a few examples of the many types of shield which may be used in heraldic art. The artist is free to choose whatever he likes and believes is best suited for a distinct representation of the arms. Everything else in his design, like helm, crest, mantling and even the charges, should be adjusted to the same style.

38. *The arms of George Washington, 1732–1799, the first President of the United States of America, which have their origin in the fourteenth century.*

39. *The arms of John Fitzgerald Kennedy, 1917–1963, the 35th President of the United States of America, granted to him by the Chief Herald of Ireland in 1961.*

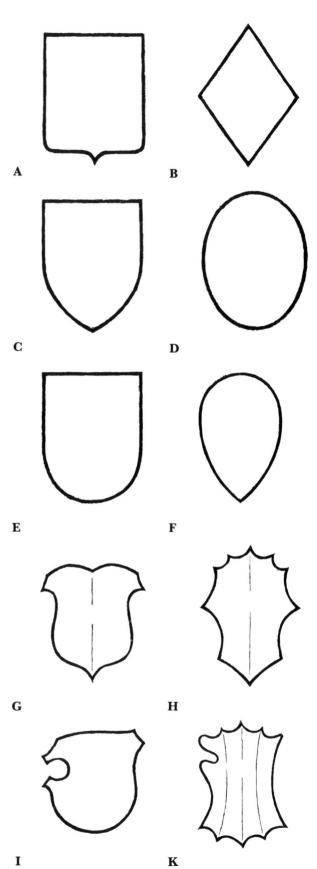

A   B

C   D

E   F

G   H

40. *Types of shield.*   I   K

THE SHIELD OR ESCUTCHEON

A. The so-called French shield actually originates from fifteenth-century Spain. It is used in the heraldry of Hungary in the second half of the seventeenth century and becomes very popular in the eighteenth century in the Netherlands, in France and in Spain. It also spreads to other countries of Europe. Its almost rectangular simplicity, in contrast to the fanciful Rococo cartouche (**Fig. 41**), suits the again growing classical taste of the period. (See **Fig. 173**.)

B. The lozenge is used as early as the thirteenth century, and in the beginning mostly by men. But since the sixteenth century it has been customary to use it as the shield for women, except in Germany and the eastern countries of Europe. (See **Figs. 235 and 294**.)

C. The almost triangular, heater-shaped shield appears in the thirteenth century. It probably is the best-liked one in heraldry and also the most characteristic of the Gothic style. (See **Figs. 174** and **175**.)

D. Oval shields (in a fancy framework) are typical of the Baroque, but are already known in the second half of the sixteenth century. Today they are normally used for the arms of women, especially if it were too difficult to squeeze the charges of the arms in a lozenge. (See **Figs. 246** and **248**.)

E. The shield which is rounded at the bottom comes originally from Spain. There, in the first half of the thirteenth century, the method of quartering is invented for which this shield is much better suited than the heater-shaped one. The custom of quartering slowly spreads all over Europe and begins to become fashionable in the fifteenth century. This is probably one of the reasons why in so many countries, from about 1500 on, this shield begins to replace the until then generally favoured Gothic shield (C).

F. This shield, still in use in Italian heraldry, is based on various shields of similar proportions from the twelfth century.

G. The greatest variety of shield-design exists in the heraldic art of the Renaissance. This is but one example from the early sixteenth century. (See **Figs. 216–221**.)

H. The horse-head shield is an invention of the Italian Renaissance and has its origin in the beginning of the sixteenth century. It is perhaps inspired by Roman shields on classical monuments or by the protective metal covering of the forehead of a knight's horse. This type of shield is still used in Italian heraldry.

I and **K.** The targe, called in British heraldry a shield à bouche, has its origin in the fourteenth century. The curved notch, cut in the dexter chief, is for the lance to pass through. The illustration on the left

41. *Rococo cartouche. (See Fig. 251.)*

(I) shows a German targe from the first half of the sixteenth century. The English one on the right (K) is from about 1450.

THE SIMPLICITY OF
EARLY HERALDRY

———— ✳ ————

42. *Senn von Munsingen, Swiss.*

43. *von Fürstenberg, German.*

44. *Atholl, Scottish.*

45. *Neville, English.*

46. *Cameron, Scottish.*

47. *Cunningham, Scottish.*

48. *Aragon, Spanish.*

49. *De Clare, English.*

50. *Campbell, Scottish.*

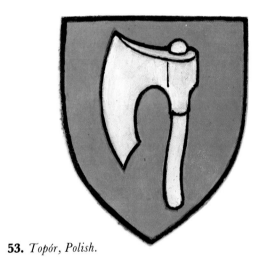

52. *Erskine, Scottish.*

53. *Topór, Polish.*

51. *The coat of arms of the von Brackel family, Baltic.*

THE MEDIEVAL COAT of arms was designed to identify a man in full armour. A knight had to be recognized in battle as a friend or a foe, not only when he was close by, but also from a greater distance. The device painted on his shield had to be simple, clear and distinct. The designer of new arms should always be aware of the original purpose of heraldry. Besides, since arms today are mainly used on signet rings and letter heads, a simple coat of arms in small size is easier to recognize than a complicated one.

We do not know the meaning behind most ancient arms. Perhaps they were chosen because they were more or less easy to paint, served the purpose and had functional appeal. Some were canting, i.e. they were related to the name of the armiger; others, for instance the eagle and the lion, could express loyalty to a suzerain, or qualities like courage, strength, magnanimity or noblesse, while a stag or antlers might have shown the armiger's love of the hunt.

54. *Burgundy, ancient.*

55. *Stewart, Scottish.*

56. *Castile.*

57. *Stafford, English.*

58. *Berlaymont, Belgian.*

59. *The Chisholm, Scottish*

60. *Spend, Danish.*

61. *Friis af Saeby, Danish.*

62. *von Wolfersdorff, German.*

63. *von Hahn, German.*

64. *von Tiesenhausen, German.*

65. *von Buttlar, German.*

66. *Monaco (House of Grimaldi).*

67. *Innes, Scottish.*

68. *von Brockdorff, German.*

69. *Bavaria (House of Wittelsbach).*

70. *d'Hemricourt, Belgian.*

71. *von Erdmannsdorff, German.*

72. *Hay, Scottish.*

73. *Mackenzie, Scottish.*

74. *Orgies, Baltic.*

75. *von Rieben, German.*

76. *von Hochberg, German.*

77. *van Gistel, Flemish.*

78. *von Hülsen, German.*

79. *von Lützow, German.*

80. *Audley, English.*

81. *d'Auxy, Belgian.*

82. *The ancient Counts of Flanders.*

VARIATIONS ON A THEME
— * —

THE CROSS

NO TWO MEN or families (depending on the different customs of the European countries) may use the same arms. This is valid also for the arms of countries, provinces, towns, organizations of all kinds and ecclesiastical heraldry. In the early periods of heraldry, however, duplication could not always be avoided. An Austrian knight of the twelfth century, for instance, had no way of knowing if his assumed arms did not perhaps exist already, let us say in Scotland or in Spain. Yet in our days there is so much information available on published and registered arms that the chance of duplication is greatly diminished. Naturally, the simplest designs have been taken long ago, and yet it is still possible to create relatively simple arms, which would qualify for the original purpose of heraldry. There is no

83. *Milano, Italy.*

84. *Pavia, Italy.*

85. *De Burgh, Irish*

86. *Messina, Italy.*

87. *Marseille, France.*

88. *de Bousies, Belgian.*

89. *Modena, Italy.*

90. *de Labeville, Belgian.*

91. *The Teutonic Order.*

92. *The Order of St. Lazarus.*

93. *Geloes, Belgian.*

94. *Canterbury, Dean and Chapter*

need whatsoever to crowd too many charges in a shield, if one considers all the possibilities of heraldic design and is a little inventive.

Figs. 83–92 show a few examples of arms with the same basic design but different because of their tinctures. More arms could be created if the field or the crosses were barry, bendy, chevronny, lozengy, checky, etc, of a fur pattern or powdered with billets, bezants, stars etc.

Also the crosses could be cotised, voided or fimbriated or, instead of having plain outlines, could be engrailed, invected, indented, wavy and so on. In addition the field as well as the cross could be charged with anything the designer finds suitable. What is said here about the cross goes also for the chief, the fess, the pale, the bend, the chevron and other ordinaries. There are also many different forms of the cross.

95. *Pope Pius III, Italian.*

43

96. *Durham, England.*

97. *Lawrence, English.*

98. *English and American Insurance Company Ltd.*

99. *Ulster Bank, Northern Ireland.*

100. *Order of the Knights Templar.*

101. *The coat of arms of the High Master of the Teutonic Order in Prussia in the fourteenth century.*

Quadrupeds too can be depicted in various tinctures, but natural colours should best be avoided. Animals could be crowned, collared, bridled, etc, and could be holding something in their claws, like a sword, a mace, a sceptre, a branch, etc. They could be shown in different poses, such as rampant, passant or statant, could be charged or strewn with small charges, like billets, crosslets or gouttes; they also could be of a fur pattern, like for instance ermine. In addition they may be armed and langued of a different tincture from their bodies. Here too are innumerable possibilities to find variations. A lion could also have two heads or a double tail. Birds may appear in any tincture used in heraldry, but natural colour should be avoided. They could be shown displayed, rising, sitting (close) and volant, with or without a crown or coronet, gorged with a collar or coronet and holding some object in their talons. They could be charged on body and wings or could be of a fur pattern, chequy, lozengy, etc; they also may be scattered with small charges like gouttes, billets, crosslets, etc, and armed and langued of a different tincture of their bodies. An eagle could also have two heads.

THE LION

102. *The ancient Kingdom of León.*

103. *Bad Münder am Deister, W. Germany.*

104. *The Belgian Province of Limburg*

105. *The House of Nassau.*

106. *Luxemburg.*

107. *Hesse, West Germany.*

108. *Orlamünde, West Germany.*

109. *Lehrte, West Germany.*

110. *County of Birkenfeld, W. Germany.*

THE EAGLE

111. *Frankfurt/Main, West Germany.*

112. *Germersheim, West Germany.*

113. *de Coligny, French.*

114. *Villingen, West Germany.*

115. *The ancient Marquisate of Moravia.*

116. *The Prince Elector of Brandenburg.*

117. *Rottweil, West Germany.*   **118.** *The ancient Duchy of Swidnizca.*   **119.** *Neuchâtel, Switzerland.*

The original attitude of the heraldic eagle was displayed, and in good heraldry its appearance is rather more stylized than true to nature.

The original attitude of the heraldic lion was rampant, and in good heraldry its appearance is rather more stylized than true to nature.
Adaptation from an illustration by René De Cramer, 1913.

STYLIZATION OF
HERALDIC CHARGES
—— ✳ ——

HERALDIC CHARGES SHOULD be stylized and photographic realism avoided. Stylization primarily depends on the prevailing taste of a period, which is easily recognizable if we compare heraldic designs of the lion and the eagle for example from various geographical areas and from different times. The often slim and sometimes elegantly grotesque lion of the Gothic and the early Renaissance has not much in common with the well-fed, pseudo-realistic beast we can often find in designs of the Baroque. The eagle, too, experienced quite a few changes over the centuries. Originally rather simple and sometimes hungry-looking, it turned during the fifteenth cen-

tury into a more majestic bird with fuller wings and tail. From the beginning on its tail feathers had been stylized, mostly similar to a fleur-de-lis upside-down, but now the tail developed into a rich ornament, sometimes of almost half the length of an eagle.

The talented artist will automatically stylize in his own manner (see **Fig. 120**), expressing things in his individual style, but he must always be aware of the heraldic character of an armorial design, which cannot be gained by approaching it with the attitude of a commercial artist designing trademarks.

120. *Stylizations.*

THE HELM
OR HELMET
———————— ✳ ————————

THE HELM OF a complete armorial display should be represented in a more or less realistic manner, i.e. the artist should strive for a slightly stylized version of a real helm.

Since helms, like shields, are of different patterns at various periods, it is important that they both are depicted in the same style. The charges of the arms are painted on the shield. Thus they become actually a painting within a painting. But helm, crest and mantling are supposed to be real, three-dimensional objects and therefore should be treated in a different way, at least from the viewpoint of the realist. The helm is usually painted in steel or silver colour and sometimes decorated with gold. Especially in France, Portugal, Spain and Italy helms are often damascened. Helms of emperors, kings and royal princes are usually painted gold. The inside of the helm is mostly lined red or purple but could also be of the first colour mentioned in the blazon.

Rightly the helm should rest on the upper edge of the shield, which can be disadvantageous to the charges, since they might get partly covered. There is, however, enough leeway given to the artist to solve this problem, as long as he sees to it that the helm does not float above the shield.

A **B** **C**

121. *Types of helm.*

49

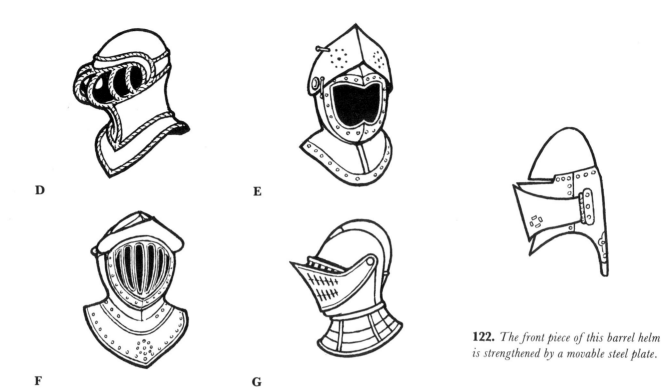

D

E

F

G

122. *The front piece of this barrel helm is strengthened by a movable steel plate.*

A. The pot helm with a flat top was the commonest type in the thirteenth century. Worn over a hood of mail, it was meant for use in action only and was at other times slung from the saddle. Crests were not in general use yet, and if there were any mantling it was normally short. (See **Fig. 174**.)

B. The barrel helm, also called great helm, made its appearance at the end of the thirteenth century. It was worn over the bascinet, a pointed steel cap, and rested on the shoulders. It was easier to attach a three-dimensional figure to its conical top than to the flat one of the pothelm, and from this time on the crest came into general use. The mantling became longer and had jagged or scalloped edges, and the crest-wreath, as we know it today, made its first appearance. (See **Fig. 179**.)

C. The tilting helm is a tournament helm which is used in the tilt or joust, in which the combatants try to unhorse each other with lances. It developed c.1400 from the barrel helm and was in use till the beginning of the sixteenth century. In heraldic design the mantling grows with this helm and slowly turns into a more and more decorative ornament. (See **Figs. 170** and **171**.)

D. Ceremonial helm from the middle of the fifteenth century. It is made of leather, painted and gilded, and has an aperture before the face, protected by bars. The bars are made of twisted rope that had been drenched in glue. On tombstones we do not find this type of helm as part of a knight's armour, but often of his coat of arms. (See **Figs. 191** and **207**.)

E. Helm with an opening before the face that can be protected by a vizor. This type of helm was in use about 1600 and could serve quite well as a model for the heraldic helm of British baronets and knights. Since baronets were first created in 1611 this helm would be appropriate. There are also similarly-formed helms which have iron bars or lattice before the aperture in addition to the vizor or attached to it. Such helms are mainly used in the heraldry of the Iberian peninsula, France and Italy. (See **Figs. 508** and **509**.)

F. Helm from the beginning of the seventeenth century. The bars are part of the vizor.

G. Type of helm from the second half of the sixteenth century with its vizor closed. Similar helms began to replace the tilting helm during the early part of that century, and soon appeared also in heraldry. (See **Fig. 207**.)

The helms described under E, F and G are from periods in which heraldic crests and mantling were in fact not in use any more or on their way out (G). If any ornament reminiscent of a crest is worn at all, it consists mainly of ostrich plumes. (See **Figs. 214** and **215**.)

THE CREST

———— ✱ ————

THE CREST, IN the days of chivalry mostly made of leather, light wood or oakum, is a decorative and identifying device which is firmly attached to the helm. This means that the artist cannot treat it like the charges in the shield, but must think of it as a three-dimensional ornament on the helm. It also means that if the helm is turned in one direction the crest cannot face another. (See **Figs. 174** and **189**.)

However, there are problems which do not make it always easy to follow common sense. In the first place there is the technical difficulty of drawing helm and crest in corresponding perspective, if the latter is for instance composed of two wings displayed (i.e. wings standing out from the helm with their pinions) and the helm, for some reason, has to be shown in profile. (The position of the helm might be fixed by some rule of paper-heraldry, while the crest depends on its description in the blazon.) In some cases a compromise is possible, but more often it is not and the artist is forced to draw the illogical combination of a helm in profile with a crest affronté.

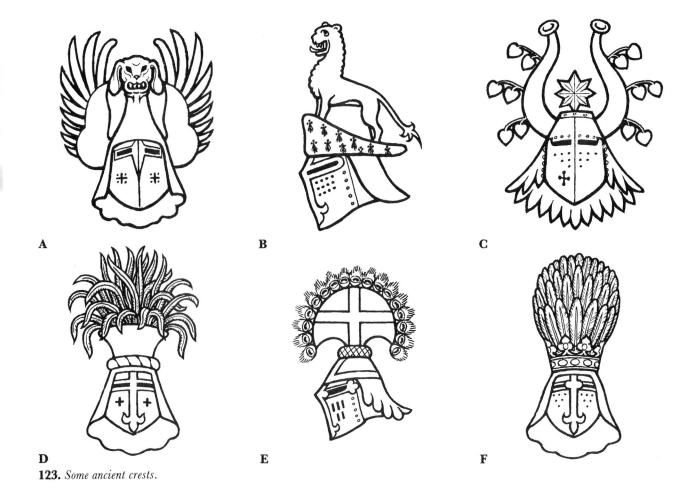

A

B

C

D

E

F

123. *Some ancient crests.*

In **Fig. 123**, the crests of A and C cannot look right if the helm is placed in profile. The wings of A, for instance, probably cut out from a light wooden plate, would appear as not much more than a vertical line*. On the other hand the profile position would be to the advantage of the dog's head.

The horns (not elephant trunks) of C, decorated with linden leaves, and the star between them present about the same problem. In both cases, if it is considered necessary, the helm could be turned sideways, but only slightly. Whether the star then could be drawn in perspective or not depends on the heraldic rules of the country from which the coat of arms originates.

In B the standing lion on the cap of maintenance looks best in profile. In an affronté position it could be difficult to show that it is not sitting.

The plate in E, decorated with the 'eyes' of peacock's feathers, would not be much more than a vertical line if the helm were drawn in an affronté position. Yet artists have ignored the direction of the real crest for a long time and such plates were drawn as seen in profile, if the helm, for some reason, had to be shown affronté.

The crests of D and F are composed of panaches (arrangements of feathers). The appearance of such

*If the blazon prescribes wings addorsed, the helm is placed best in three-quarters profile.

crests does not change if the helm is turned in a different direction.

Another problem arises when for instance the crest should consist of a lion rampant between two wings displayed. The wings look best on a helm affronté, but the lion would not only be very difficult to draw in the same perspective; it would in addition not correspond to the lion rampant prescribed in the blazon. In such a case the best solution is probably to draw the helm in a three-quarters profile position and ajdust the crest to it. With the helm in three-quarters profile (**Figs. 124** and **125**) it is still possible to show the position of the wings correctly.

The main reason why the front view of an animal is disliked in heraldry is obviously the fact that it is in most cases much more difficult to draw, while the profile usually gives the artist a chance to be more distinct in emphasizing its characteristic features. But one should not forget that the real crest-figures were three-dimensional and could be seen from different angles. It is also quite improbable that in the early days of heraldry a crest-figure would have normally looked any other way but forward.

Figs. 126–128 show types of crest which should always be depicted in profile or three-quarters profile, since a frontal view would neither be beneficial to their looks nor to their heraldic accuracy.

124. *Wings displayed.*

125. *Wings addorsed.*

126. *The coat of arms of Derk Kinnane Roelofsma, Paris, France, an American of Dutch and Irish descent.*

127. *The coat of arms of the German family Reidemeister (according to Siebmacher).*

128. *The coat of arms of Manuel Artur Norton, Baron de São Roque, Povoa de Lanhoso, Portugal.*

THE TORSE
OR CREST-WREATH
————— * —————

THE TORSE OR crest-wreath is represented as a twisted piece of cloth of two tinctures, in continental heraldry sometimes more, which appear alternately in the folds. Unless other tinctures are specified, the torse is like the mantling of the principal colour and metal of the arms. In British heraldry six folds are visible in representation, of which the first on the dexter side is of metal. In the heraldry of other countries the number of folds is unimportant but is normally five. In Italian heraldry for instance the cloth is so tightly twisted that eight or more folds are pos-

sible, and the torse, being actually an alternative to the crest-coronet and the chapeau, may serve as the basis for a coronet to rest upon.

In the heraldry of Great Britain the torse is a must, while in other countries, Switzerland or Germany for instance, it could be left out, especially if the material of the crest-figure could easily be continued into the mantling. In such a case, if the tincture of the crest were metal, the outside of the mantling would automatically also be of metal.

129. *Arms of the German family von Gordon, descending from Sir John Gordon of Strathbogie, died c.1394.*

130. *The Swedish arms of the Finnish heraldic artist Gustav von Numers. Crest-wreath and mantling are of two colours and one metal. The badge of a knight of honour of the Order of St John (Johanniterorden) is suspended from the shield.*

131. *The ancient arms of the German dynastic family von Metternich. No torse or crest-coronet are used. The crest is placed like a hood on the helm, its material continuing to form the mantling.*

132. *Arms of Hans Burgkmair, German painter and graphic artist, 1473–1531. The arms were probably granted in 1516. Adaptation from his own design.*

THE CAP OF
MAINTENANCE
& OTHER HATS
———— * ————

THE CHAPEAU OR cap of maintenance (**Fig. 133**) is an alternative to the torse and the crest-coronet. It has been limited in modern times in Great Britain to peers and to territorial barons in Scotland. The latter may place it above the shield like a coronet of rank. This cap of dignity is tinctured gules and turned-up ermine. If a Scottish baron is not in the possession of his barony any more, but still uses the territorial designation, the cap is azure, turned-up ermine.

In continental heraldry various shapes of hat are used (see **Figs. 134–138**). Some of them might have been status symbols long ago, as the princely and ducal bonnets still are.

133. *Chapeau or cap of maintenance as used in British heraldry.*

134. *von Keudell, German.*

135. *Neuhoff gen. von der Ley, German.*

136. *von Gersdorff, German.*

137. *von Vietinghoff gen. Scheel, German.*

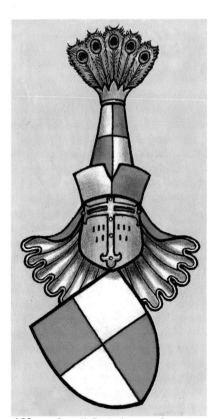

138. *zu Castell-Rüdenhausen, German.*

CREST-CORONETS & CORONETS OF RANK

CROWNS AND CORONETS should be placed firmly on the shield or helm and not float above them. If a coronet of rank has to be placed on a helm which is shown in three-quarters profile, it is better not adjusted to this position, unless it still clearly indicates the rank it stands for.

The crest-coronet, which in British heraldry is misleadingly called ducal coronet, descends from the crowns which kings and princes would wear on their helms during the thirteenth century. They were circlets heightened with ornaments of various floral and foliated forms. However, in the fourteenth

139. *von Rauchhaupt, German. In several countries this type of coronet may be placed on the shield by the untitled nobility.*

140. *This crest-coronet is often used by the nobility of all ranks in several European countries.*

141. *The coat of arms of the ancient German von Arnim family. In an armorial design based on the Gothic style, the crest-coronet should be used only if it was already part of the coat of arms in the fourteenth century.*

142. *Coronets of rank.*

century, this symbol of high leadership had already lost its original meaning and we find it from then on used by many noblemen of all different ranks as an alternative to the torse, sometimes even tinctured red or blue. In modern times it is normally depicted in gold with three visible strawberry or acanthus leaves and points between them, which are often topped with a pearl or a silver ball.

Occasionally the crest-coronet appears in burgher arms, which is correct only if the arms were granted by a sovereign and the coronet is explicitly mentioned in the grant.

The circlet of the majority of coronets of rank (see **Fig. 142**) is heightened either with pearls or leaves (stylized acanthus or strawberry) or with a combination of both. Their arrangement and number is significant for the rank they represent. Every country has its own system and sometimes two or more coronets for the same nobiliary rank. Most circlets are jewelled. Coronets of British peers are the exception: their circlets are not actually gemmed but chased as jewelled.

A. A coronet with five visible leaves could belong to a duke, a prince, a marquis or a count, depending on which time and country his title originates from. In the modern heraldic crown of a king the arches normally rise from five leaves. The British royal crown is an exception, since it has only three visible arches which rise from crosses patté. (See **Figs. 423** and **264**.)

B. Typical coronet of a marquis, as used in countries of the Romance languages and in Belgium.

C. Coronet of a Swedish baron.

D. Coronet for a baron in the heraldry of several countries.

E. Coronet of a Burggraaf (viscount) in Dutch heraldry.

F. Coronet of a viscount in the heraldry of several countries.

G. The tortil, a circlet entwined by a string of pearls of which three or four strands are visible, is used for barons in the heraldry of several countries.

H. Coronet for a Knight (noble title) in Belgium and the Netherlands. It may also be used by untitled nobles in the Netherlands.

Most coronets of rank have their origin in the seventeenth century, and the custom to place them between shield and helm dates from about the same period. From the purist's point of view this procedure can hardly be looked upon as good heraldry, yet it seems to be still widely accepted and quite normal in the official heraldry of Great Britain and Belgium. (See **Fig. 29**.)

Normally the coronet of rank should rest on the shield only if the helm is not used, in which case the crest should not rise from it. In Sweden, France, Portugal, Spain and Italy it is customary today to place the coronet of rank also on the helm. (See **Fig. 128**.)

Coronets of British peers are worn about a crimson cap with a gold tassel and guarded with ermine. After 1814 the coronets of pairs de France were depicted with a blue cap with a gold tassel and trimmed with ermine. Spanish grandees place a red cap with a gold ball inside their coronet. The reader searching for a particular crown, crest-coronet or coronet of rank is referred to the author's book *Heraldry: Customs, Rules and Styles* which was first published by Blandford Press in 1981.

143. *The armorial bearings of the Belgian Counts de la Serna de la Laguna de Terminos (of Spanish origin). The shield is ensigned with the coronet of nine pearls, which is probably the internationally best known, since it is recognized in at least ten countries as the coronet for a count.*

144. *Coronet for a British marquess.*

145. *Coronet for a British duke.*

THE MANTLING

THE MANTLING OR Lambrequin must be fashioned in the style of shield and helm and should have a three-dimensional effect. If only the shield is used, it should never be adorned by mantling, and to depict the crested helm of an achievement without it is equally wrong. The mantling is usually kept in two tinctures which are the same as the main colour and metal of the arms mentioned first in the blazon. The metal is normally the tincture of the lining. However, there are a great number of coat of arms in European heraldry which have more than two tinctures in their mantling. We quite often find, especially in Hungarian arms, mantlings which are on one side argent and azure, and on the other Or and gules, even if the shield should have one colour and one metal only. In Italy, Spain and France it can happen that all the tinctures contained in the arms appear also in the mantling, while Scottish peers use red mantling lined with ermine, regardless of the tinctures in their arms.

146. *Types of mantling.*

German,
1589.

Danish,
1701.

German,
1589.

Russian,
1796.

146. *Types of mantling.*

147. *Stirling of Calder, Scotland. In the fourteenth century mantling began to be represented sometimes as ending in gold tassels. They still may be used in modern heraldry.*

Mantling was sometimes strewn with charges of the arms or could be semé of anything lending itself to such treatment. It could even be charged with the arms. With the mantling getting more and more stylized and (especially during the Renaissance and the Baroque) looking often more like dense foliage than a piece of cloth, it became difficult for artists, in some cases impossible, to apply such ornaments. Mantlings charged with anything at all are rare in modern heraldry.

During the thirteenth and fourteenth centuries it was fashionable to adorn horse-equipment with jingle bells, which soon appeared on the clothing of noblemen and were also used on crests and mantlings. Could it be that the bezants, strewn on the mantling of some ancient coats of arms, were originally such bells?

The tinctures of the mantling should always be mentioned in the blazon, since it cannot be taken for granted that they are of the two main tinctures of the shield.

148. *The coat of arms of the Count de Nesles, France.*

149. *The coat of arms of Bruce, Lord of Annandale, Scotland.*

MANTEAU & ROBE OF ESTATE

————— ✳ —————

THE HERALDIC MANTEAU is not an article of clothing but has in all probability its origin in the draperies around a throne. The custom of placing the arms of kings and princes on a manteau spread during the seventeenth century all over Europe, after a French engraver had erroneously given the impression that the arms of the King of France were displayed under a tent. The manteau and the heraldic tent with a cupola, called pavilion, have since been used by princes and the high nobility in Europe, excepting Great Britain and Ireland.

Manteau and pavilion were normally purple with golden bordures, fringes and tassels. Today they are often depicted as red, even if the blazon describes them as purpure. (See **Figs. 257, 258** and **264**.)

They are usually lined with ermine, though there are exceptions. The heraldic mantle of Italian titular princes and dukes, for instance, is according to the last official rulings (1943) supposed to be purpure (in practice mostly red) without any tassels or fringes. The lining is of white ermine but without the black ermine tails. These manteaux do not necessarily have to be topped by a crown or a coronet of rank but may be shown as coming from under the crested helm with its mantling, which gives the impression of a real robe of estate. This term used in British heraldry to describe the manteau could also correctly be used for manteaux which are on the outside decorated with the charges of the shield, and probably descend from mantles that were really worn in the Middle Ages by people of high social standing. (See **Fig. 184.**)

Manteaux may also be blue, like the one of a Pair de France or a royal Prince of Sweden. The Order of Malta uses a black one to symbolize its spiritual character (see **Fig. 388**). Sometimes manteaux and pavilions are strewn with charges of the arms or with badges. Thus, the blue manteau of the King of France was semé de lis, while the Emperor Napoleon I used golden bees. The red pavilion of the King of Italy was scattered with little silver crosses and the golden one of the German Emperors (House of Hohenzollern) with black eagles and imperial crowns.

150. *The arms of the Russian Princes Kropotkin, descending from Dmitri Kropotka, c.1450, Prince of Smolensk. Not only the shield but also a complete achievement could be displayed on a manteau.*

151. *This pattern for the arms of a titular Italian Prince or Duke has a manteau that reminds of a real mantle or robe of estate.*

SUPPORTERS

———— * ————

SUPPORTERS PROBABLY HAVE their origin in the purely decorative figures which were used by engravers, without any heraldic intention, to fill the empty space on a seal between the inscription around its edge and the coat of arms in the middle. In armorial designs supporters began to be used in the late fourteenth century, but more as artistic trimmings to the overall composition and not yet as fixed heraldic devices. Sometimes they might have had a special meaning, yet the true supporter emerged in the middle of the fifteenth century.

Supporters should be kept heraldic in character but also three-dimensional in effect (See **Figs. 246** to **249**.) They should stand on a compartment or some architectural pediment, but having them balance on the scroll of a motto should be avoided. The compartment can be used for the display of badges.

152. *The arms of the Belgian Barons de Potesta de Waleffe.*

MOTTO
&
BANNERS

———— ✳ ————

Arms of Edward Irving of Bonshaw, clan chief in the 16th century. The arms were recorded by his heir-male in the New Lyon Register c 1672. The basic arms of the clan.

153. *The coat of arms of Ian Grant, Edinburgh, Scotland.*

154. *Schwenkelbanner. The ancient German Reichssturmfahne (after F. Warnecke).*

155. *Banner with the arms of Brabant.*

THE MOTTO IS usually written in black letters on a white scroll or riband which is placed below the shield. It may be in any language. It may express in a brief, striking phrase some pious or idealistic sentiment, or play on the name of the bearer. Only in Scotland, where it is placed above the crest, is it a necessary part of a coat of arms. In continental heraldry it is sometimes kept in the livery colours, the scroll in the colour, its back and the letters in the metal of the mantling, or the back of the white riband with black letters is painted in the main colours of the arms. A cri de guerre (war cry) is always placed on a scroll above the crest. It is mostly found in French heraldry. (See **Fig. 286**.)

Banners appear sometimes in combination with armorial bearings of kings, princes, the titled nobility and civic authorities. The field of such a banner is identical to the field of the shield. If the shield is flanked by two supporters holding banners then the one on dexter is turned around, so that its charges are seen in reverse. This is according to the rule (not accepted everywhere) that dexter of an heraldic flag is in the hoist, i.e. next to the stave, while sinister is in the fly. (See **Figs. 346** and **347**.)

ECCLESIASTICAL HERALDRY

———— ✳ ————

IN ECCLESIASTICAL HERALDRY the insignia of office and rank in the hierarchy of the Roman Catholic Church are the tiara of the Pope, the bishops' mitre, the flat prelates' hat with its cord and tassels, the crossed keys of the Pope, the crozier or pastoral staff and the cross-staff.

In modern heraldry only the prelates' hat is placed above the shield of a clergyman. Its colour and the number of tassels show the rank of its owner.

Archbishops place a cross-staff with two bars behind their shield, bishops a staff with the simple cross, abbots a crozier with a veil.

Dioceses and abbeys may ensign their shield respectively with mitre, cross and crozier or mitre and crozier with a veil.

In the heraldry of the Anglican Church all bishops ensign their arms with a mitre and may place two croziers in saltire behind their shield.

Bishops of the American Episcopal Church also use the mitre. They may place a golden key and crozier crossed in saltire, behind the shield.

A black prelates' hat with cord and tassels in different colours, to distinguish position and office in the hierarchy of the church, may be used in both churches to replace helm and crest of a clergyman's arms. Mitre, cross-staff and crozier are also used by a few other Protestant churches.

For a detailed study of Church heraldry the author recommends the standard work *Heraldry in the Catholic Church, its Origins, Customs and Laws*, by Bruno Bernard Heim, Van Duren, Gerrards Cross, England, second edition, 1981. In this lavishly-illustrated book the student will find also a chapter on the heraldry in the oriental churches in union with the Holy See, the heraldry in the Church of England and the Church of Scotland.

The basic colour of the mitre is in modern times always gold or white and may be enriched by diapering. Also, the mitre may be jewelled or chased as jewelled. In the heraldry of the Catholic Church it must be lined red, and the inside of the ribbons depending from the back should be red too.

156. *The arms of Pope John Paul II (elected in 1978). The shield is ensigned with the tiara, the special crown of the Pope and the emblem of the Papacy. The keys of St Peter are crossed in saltire behind the shield and are linked by a red cord with two tassels. The keys could also be placed above the shield. This is the typical composition of a pope's coat of arms, and it is not permissible to add any exterior ornaments or decorations.*

157. *Designs like this for the arms of bishops were quite normal in former times. In this particular case the sword symbolizes temporal power. Today, however, the arms of a Catholic clergyman are composed as in Figs. 159 and 160.*

158. *The arms of an abbot were usually designed in this manner. Nowadays this would suggest the arms of an abbey. The arms of an abbot should be designed as in Fig. 160 but with the veiled crozier behind the shield instead of the cross-staff. Hat, cord and tassels are black for an abbot and green for an abbot nullius.*

159. *Pattern for the arms of an archbishop of the Catholic Church. Hat, cord and tassels are green. Cardinals use a red hat with 15 red tassels hanging from a red cord on either side of the shield.*

160. *Pattern for the arms of a bishop of the Catholic Church. Hat, cord and tassels are green. A simple priest ensigns his shield with a black hat with black cord and one black tassel on either side of the shield.*

161. *The arms of Dr Bengt Sundkler, a Swede, Bishop of Bokuba in the Evangelical Church of North-West Tanganjika, Africa, 1961.*

162. *The arms of an Anglican bishop, the Bishop of Salisbury, England.*

163. *The arms of Monsignor Bruno Bernard Heim, titular Archbishop of Xanthus, Apostolic Delegate in London. (see* **Fig. 382.***)*

164. *(Left) Arms of the Bishop in charge of the Convocation of American Churches in Europe. Normally bishops of the Episcopal Church place a golden key and a crozier in saltire behind the shield. These were left out here for artistic reasons. The key and crozier are objects of quite different sizes. In their true relationship to each other, the key would not even be seen behind the shield. The arms were originally designed by Derk Kinnane Roelofsma, Paris, France, in consultation with Cecil R. Humphery-Smith, Canterbury, Kent, England.*

165. *Arms of the Dean of the American Cathedral (dedicated to the Holy Trinity) in Paris, France. The shield is ensigned with the hat of an Anglican dean. The original design is by Derk Kinnane Roelofsma in consultation with the author.*

166. *The arms of the Episcopalian Diocese of El Camino Real, Monterey, California, USA. The original design is by the Rev. John Andrew, D.D., New York, in consultation with the author.*

VARIOUS APPROACHES TO THE DESIGN OF A COAT OF ARMS

———— ✳ ————

167 *and* **168.** *The coat of arms of the Loutsch family of Luxemburg, according to the 'Armorial du Pays de Luxembourg' by Dr Jean-Claude Loutsch, 1974. Two different designs by the author, Antwerp, 1982. Arms: Parted per pale; Dexter, argent, three piles issuing from the dexter traversé barwise sable, the middle pile between two crosslets gules. Sinister, barry of six, azure and argent. Crest: Out of a crest-coronet two eagle's wings displayed, the dexter argent, the sinister azure. Mantling: Dexter, sable lined argent; sinister, azure lined argent.*

169. *Blazon of the coat of arms of Peter Bander van Duren, of Gerrards Cross, Buckinghamshire, England.*

Arms: Quarterly, 1 and 4: Or, a lion rampant gules armed, langued and crowned with a coronet of a ridder (knight) of the Netherlands azure; 2 and 3: Argent, two bars sable, on a chief of the last two mullets of the field, all within a bordure quarterly sable and gules.

Crest: A demi lion gules, armed and langued and crowned with a coronet as in the arms azure, holding aloft by the dexter paw two keys saltirewise, one Or surmounting the other argent, interlaced at the bows by a cord gules.

Motto: EN DIEU EST MON ESPERANCE ('My hope is in God').

HERALDRY IS AN art and a science. I mention the art first since the pictorial representation is essential for the existence of the science. On the other hand, the art of heraldry depends on particular heraldic rules and customs and, like all other art-forms, on the ability of the artist.

In the blazon, the verbal description of a coat of arms, the charges of the shield, their tinctures and position, the crest, the mantling and other appurtenances are given. The artist must make his design by strictly following this verbal description.

But, since only the contents of the armorial bearings are pinned down in the blazon and not their artistic form, his talent, craftsmanship and inventiveness are solely responsible for the artistic character and value of the design. We may not say for its beauty, since the composition (the contents and their arrangement) of some coats of arms is so unartistic that even the best designer, being bound to the given and unchangeable facts of the blazon, might not be able to create an appealing picture. Every artist-designer has his own handwriting, his own aesthetic feelings, his own style. He cannot be criticised for the heraldic musts, unless he is creating an entirely new armorial achievement. Thus, it is only his transforming of a text into a drawing, painting or sculpture etc, his subjective artistic interpretation, that he has to answer for.

There are people who always copy faithfully the original design of arms from a grant or a painting, which has been for several generations in the family, perhaps to avoid mistakes, but more often probably because it is easier to copy than to create. Thus, many armigers came to believe that their armorial bearings were depicted incorrectly if the designer deviated in his work from the pattern they were used to. Compare **Figs. 130** and **440**, **1** and **518**, **163** and **382**, **385** and **423**.

PART II
*
HERALDIC ART
& CRAFT
OVER THE CENTURIES
*

STYLES OF ARCHITECTURE & ART WHICH HAVE INFLUENCED HERALDIC DESIGN

THESE STYLES DEVELOPED national and regional features and did not fully correspond in the different European countries, either in their duration or in their artistic expression and form. They usually relieved one another slowly, often overlapping or even blending. Thus, the student should be warned that it is not safe to generalize too much about styles and periods. We find always exceptions which would not fit into the overall pattern. With that reservation in mind the generalizations of a table of styles may be accepted, since they can give us a general concept of certain periods and a foothold in the flux of historic development.

THE GOTHIC STYLE, from about 1150 to 1530.
EARLY GOTHIC, from about 1150 to 1220/50.
EARLY ENGLISH, thirteenth century.
HIGH GOTHIC, from about 1220/50 to 1350/70.
DECORATED STYLE in England, fourteenth century.
INTERNATIONAL GOTHIC STYLE, around 1400.
LATE GOTHIC, from about 1350/70 to 1530.
PERPENDICULAR STYLE in England, fifteenth century.

TUDOR STYLE in England, from 1485 to c.1560, basically medieval but showing first signs of classical decoration.
PLATERESCO or PLATERESQUE STYLE in Spain, a combination of late Gothic and early Renaissance in which Moorish elements were blended. It lasted until about 1556.
ELIZABETHAN/JACOBEAN, from about 1560 to 1620, a transitional period between the Gothic and the Renaissance in England.

RENAISSANCE, from about 1400 to 1600.
EARLY RENAISSANCE, only in Italy (QUATRO-
CENTO), from about 1400 to 1500.
HIGH RENAISSANCE, in Italy (CINQUE-
CENTO), from 1500 to 1560.
MANNERISM =LATE RENAISSANCE, from 1530 to 1600.

BAROQUE, from about 1600 to the first third of the eighteenth century.
ROCOCO, the playful and decadent end of the Baroque, from about 1740 to 1770.

CLASSICISM, from about 1760/70 to c. 1840.
EMPIRE, the style of the empire of Napoleon I, influenced by the style of the Imperium Romanum.

ROMANTICISM, from the late eighteenth to the second half of the nineteenth century.

INTRODUCTION

———— ✳ ————

THE STUDY OF heraldic art requires the study of the styles of art and craft which have been essentially influential on its development over the centuries. The student should also get acquainted with the military armament of the first four hundred years of heraldry's existence, particularly with the different types of shield and helm. Also, some knowledge of the spirit of the various historical periods, their fine art, architecture and even costumology can add to a greater awareness and a deeper understanding of the characteristic features of heraldic art and the changes it underwent in the course of time. A synoptical approach to the subject can make the experience richer, more exciting and inspiring. It is not really too far-fetched if we see a relationship between the heater-shaped shield and the pointed arch of Gothic architecture, or the full-bottomed wig of the Baroque and an heraldic cartouche.

The periods of the Gothic style and the early Renaissance are the most important. This was the age when heraldry was in its blossom, when it was part of everyday life and in practical use as never again in later centuries. We find the best examples of artistic skill and inventiveness in seals, coins, in illuminated manuscripts, on tombs and monuments of stone and metal and in stained-glass windows. Early rolls of arms were not necessarily meant to be pieces of art and we must consider them in the first place as records.

They were in general the work of heralds or of expert amateurs. Some of them, however, contain truly artistic designs and/or reflect strongly the heraldic spirit of the period, as for example the *Armorial Bellenville* (circa 1364–1386), the *Armorial de Gelre* (1370–1386) or the *Armorial Equestre de la Toison d'Or et de l'Europe* (from about the middle of the fifteenth century), to mention but three.

The decline of the art began already in the sixteenth century, when heraldry became slowly detached from the theme of the reason for its arising. Shield, helm and mantling, not real objects to the artist any more, would be treated in a more or less imaginative and ornamental manner. Also, the realism of Renaissance art with perspective and shading had invaded heraldry, and the difference between on the one hand shield and helm as three-dimensional and on the other the charges on the shield as flat objects was soon forgotten. Another important reason for the decadence of heraldry must have been the almost contemptuous attitude of the Renaissance mind towards the Gothic, which had received its derogatory name, meaning barbarian, from the Italian art world of the sixteenth century. There was no appreciation of the period in neo-classic thinking or feeling.

During the Baroque heraldic art became even more estranged from its beginnings. This style had evolved from the Renaissance in sixteenth-century Italy under the influence of the last works of Michelangelo. In the seventeenth century it spread to all the countries of Europe. Its generally elaborate and sometimes grotesque ornamentation made heraldic design often look very decorative and impressive, but the medieval spirit had disappeared. In newly-created arms the taboo on natural colours for charges on the shield was not always respected, and many of these arms had been designed with quarterings containing symbolic allusions, but without any genealogical meaning. The oval shield in an ornate frame, the pavilion and the manteau, the latter new accessories to princely arms, are typical creations of paper heraldry and an expression of the often theatrical splendour of the Baroque.

We may see the Rococo as the slightly decadent and elegant last phase of the Baroque. Ornament of pierced shellwork and fanciful curved forms are characteristic of the style. The oval Rococo shield of heraldry is mostly shown in a slanting position and surrounded by informally balanced scroll-work and flowers. It is often ensigned with a coronet, balancing on top of the ornamental frame. By the eighteenth century the interest in heraldry had noticeably lessened. Heraldic sculpture, still found quite often on Baroque buildings, became extremely rare

170 and **171**. *The arms of Ortenburg and Dalmatia at the time of the brothers Frederick II and Ulrich II, both Counts of Cilly. In 1430 they had been granted princely privileges and rights by Emperor Sigismund and governed together Dalmatia,* *Croatia and Slavonia, bearing the title of Princely Counts at Cilly, Ortenburg and Segoria. From the MS Cod. 255,* Complainte des hérauts d'armes, *middle of the fifteenth century, in the City Library of Antwerp, Belgium.*

in the Rococo. The coat of arms as a meaningful ornament in the background of a portrait had already lost its popularity, and noblemen frequently preferred a fancy design of their initials, topped by their coronet of rank, to decorate their personal belongings.

By the end of that period heraldry had reached its lowest level. The classical spirit of the Renaissance, which had lingered on during the Baroque and the Rococo, had begun to gain predominance again. Classicism, a cool and formal style experienced through archaeological research and the knowledge of the ancient cultures of Greece and Rome, spread over Europe and America. Classical forms were used everywhere and in every possible way.

Attempts to adjust heraldry to this dominating style normally ended in lamentable results.

Under Napoleon I a new standardized heraldic system was devised, that was supposed to reflect the hierarchy of the French empire. It had not very much in common with traditional heraldry, neither in spirit nor in form. But, being a creation of the period, its formal designs were naturally well adapted to the style of contemporary architecture and crafts. After the downfall of Napoleon I it disappeared from the scene and had only a short revival under Napoleon III. This marginal phenomenon had no influence on the further development of heraldic art.

Romanticism, an emotional style in reactionary

172. *The arms of Alphonsus de Berges, Archbishop of Mechlin, who died in 1689. Stone carving in the style of the Baroque (with classical features) in St Rombouts Cathedral, Mechlin, Belgium.*

173. *The arms of Jean-Jacques, duc de Cambacéres, Archichancelier de l'Empire, who died in 1824; from the coffin trappings used at his funeral. According to the rules of Napoleonic heraldry the design is not completely correct, but nevertheless demonstrates how far heraldry had deviated from its original course. From the collection of M. Gaston Saffroy, Paris, France.*

position to the formality and the academic conservatism of Classicism, found its ideals in history and literature. It brought forth a new interest in the Middle Ages, which eventually also caused a reawakening of the interest in heraldry.

The quickly-changing styles of art from the second half of the nineteenth century on were of no influence, though around the turn of the century the presence of Art Nouveau, and a little later of Expressionism, could occasionally be felt in heraldic design. In general, however, a certain eclecticism was the norm, in which Gothic, Renaissance and early Baroque elements were freely mixed. On the other hand, one began to accept the Gothic style and the early Renaissance as authoritative standards.

THIRTEENTH & FOURTEENTH CENTURIES

*

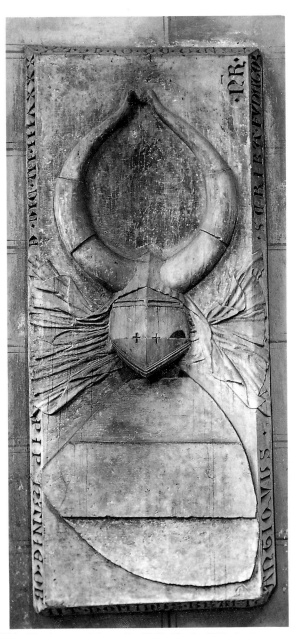

174. *Tombstone of the scribe N.N. Kraft, 1298, in the Dreifaltigkeits Kirche (Church of the Holy Trinity) in Ulm, Württemberg, West Germany.*

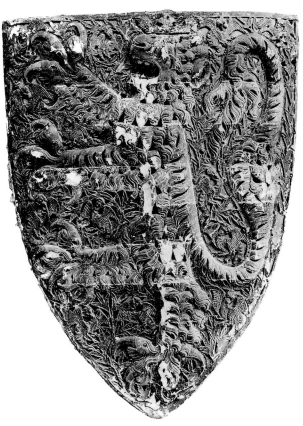

175. *Shield of Henry I, Landgrave of Hesse, 1244–1308, from c.1300, made of linden wood which is partly covered with leather, partly with canvas, painted and gilded. 75.5 × 56.11 cm.*

177. *Shield with unidentified arms (Gules, an eagle displayed argent) from the St Elizabeth Church in Marburg, Hesse, c.1300, now in the University Museum.*

176. *Effigy of a Cantwell knight from Kilfane, Co. Kilkenny, Ireland, from the end of the thirteenth century.*

178. *Seal of Otto, Duke of Carinthia, Count of Tirol and Gorizia, traceable from 1296 to 1310. The arms of Carinthia appear on the shield and the neck of the horse's trapper, the arms of Tirol on the banner and the back of the trapper.*

179. *Seal of Rudolf IV, Duke of Austria, with the arms of Austria on the shield and the arms of Tirol on the banner, from 1364/1365.*

Figs. 178 and 179 are from *Das Tiroler Landeswappen*, by Franz-Heinz von Hye, Innsbruck 1972.

FIFTEENTH CENTURY

---- * ----

180. *The coat of arms of Philip the Good, Duke of Burgundy, Brabant and Limburg, Count of Flanders, Artois, etc, founder and first sovereign head of the Order of the Golden Fleece, 1396–1469. The arms are quartered of: 1 and 4, Burgundy modern, 2, per pale Burgundy ancient and Brabant, 3, per pale Burgundy ancient and Limburg; overall an inescutcheon of Flanders.*

181. *The coat of arms of Hue de Lannoy, Seigneur of Santes, c. 1384–1456. The entire achievement, even the jewel of the Golden Fleece, is contourné since the design occupies a left page. The colours are faded, because the lions of the shield should be green.*

Figs. 180–185 are illustrations from a fifteenth-century manuscript in the City Library of Antwerp, Belgium, *Complainte des hérauts d'armes* Cod. 255 B 89420, A. Dermul, Catalogue des manuscripts, 1939.

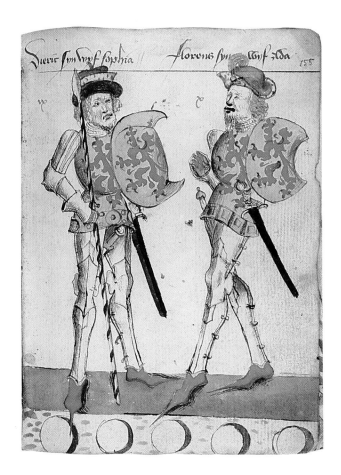

182. *Fictitious portraits of Diederik VI, Count of Holland (1122–1157) and his son and successor Floris III, Count of Holland (1157–1190). The arms attributed to the two counts in this picture, the lion of Holland, actually appear for the first time on a seal of Diederik VII in 1198.*

183. *The arms of the Silesian Duchy of Brieg, the Kingdom of Bohemia, the Principality of Schweidnitz and the Duchy of Braunschweig.*

184. *Duke Johan of Bavaria-Straubing, Count of Hainaut, Holland, Zealand and Frisia (1418–1425) and his brother's daughter Jacoba of Bavaria. The duke is carrying a targe. The type of hat he is wearing was the forerunner of the hats which were used much later in heraldry by people of princely status. The type of cloak his niece is wearing was, from the seventeenth century onwards, frequently used as a background to the arms of the high nobility. (See Figs. 232 and 233.)*

185. *The coat of arms of the Counts of Hainaut, Holland, Zealand and Frisia between the shields of Bavaria (Louis of Bavaria, Roman Emperor), Habsburg (Rudolf von Habsburg, Roman King), Hainaut and Holland, and France.*

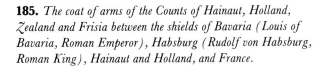

186. *Heraldic image of the emperor of the Holy Roman Empire (Imperator Romanus semper Augustus) from the* Armorial Equestre de la Toison d'Or et de l'Europe.

187. *Heraldic image of the King of England in the* Armorial Equestre de la Toison d'Or et de l'Europe *by probably Jean Lefèvre, sire de Saint Rémy (1396–1468), roi d'armes Toison d'Or. Bibliothèque de l'Arsenal in Paris, France.*

188. *Heraldic image of Robert de Masmines, Lord of Beerlegem, Hemelveerdegem and Uitbergen. He was knighted by Philip the Good, Duke of Burgundy, and died in battle at the siege of Melun in 1431. From the* Armorial Equestre de la Toison d'Or et de l'Europe. *The pages of the armorial have been slightly damaged over the centuries and have been trimmed around the edges.*

189. *Heraldic image of Jehan de Villiers, Seigneur de l'Isle-Adam, from the* Armorial Equestre de la Toison d'Or et de l'Europe. *Jehan de Villiers was a Marshal of France and defended Paris against Jeanne d'Arc in 1429. He was received into the Order of the Golden Fleece in 1430 and died in Bruges in 1437. A member of the same family was Philip Villiers de l'Isle-Adam, Grand Master of the Order of St John of Jerusalem from 1521 to 1534. Under his leadership the Knights occupied Malta in 1530, seven years after they had lost Rhodes.*

190. *Stone relief above the south portal of the church of Sterzing, Tirol, with the arms of King Maximilan I and Austria and Tirol from 1497. From* Das Tiroler Landeswappen.

192. *Effigy of Jörg Truchsess von Waldburg (died in 1467) in the church of Waldsee, Baden-Württemberg.*

191. *Stove tile from about 1450 in the Castle of Merano, South Tirol, Italy, with the coat of arms of Austria and the shields of Tirol and Merano. From* Das Tiroler Landeswappen.

193. *The coat of arms of Pierre Lanchals, Kt., counsellor of Maximilian of Austria and comptroller of his estates and finances, on his monument in the Church of Our Lady in Bruges, Belgium. Since he was loyal to his prince he was beheaded on the main square of Bruges by the rebellious populace of the city in 1488. The helm of the coat of arms had originally bars which have been broken off.*

194. *Marble relief above the main entrance of Sigmundskron Castle in Tirol from 1474. The angel supporter seems to stress the point that Austria and Tirol belong together. From* Das Tiroler Landeswappen.

195. *The coat of arms of Maximilian Archduke of Austria, who two years later became Roman Emperor, the Order's first sovereign head of the House of Habsburg, 1459–1519.*

197. *The coat of arms of Philip of Burgundy, Seigneur of Beveren, died 1498.*

196. *The coat of arms of Philip the Handsome, Archduke of Austria, Duke of Burgundy and Count of Charolais, 1478–1506. The Order of the Golden Fleece was founded by Philip the Good, Duke of Burgundy, in 1430. Its members were elected at the chapter meetings. The first chapter of the Order was held in Lille, 1431, the last one in Ghent in 1559.*

Note that in the two paintings in **Figs. 197** and **199** not only are helms and crests turned to the right to face the altar, but also the Golden Fleece.

Figs.195–199 are stall plates of Knights of the Order of the Golden Fleece in St Rombouts Cathedral, Mechlin, Belgium, where in 1491 the Order's 15th chapter was held.

198. *The coat of arms of Jean, Seigneur of Lannoy,*
1410–1493.

199. *The coat of arms of Martin, Seigneur of Polheim, died*
1498.

SIXTEENTH CENTURY

———— ✳ ————

200. *Tombstone of a member of the von Habsberg family from 1500 in the Church of St Emmeran in Regensburg, Bavaria, West Germany. To the left of the crest is the collar of the Order of St Sebastian, to the right the collar of the Crown, a tournament society.*

201. *Arms of marriage on a memorial of Georg Gollenprat von Hohenfreiberg and his wife Radegunda Eggenberger from 1512. Carthusian Monastery in Buxheim, near Memmingen, Württemberg, West Germany.*

ESPECIALLY FROM THE late Middle Ages to the Baroque we find that portrait and heraldry were closely linked together in the sculpture of monuments, in painting, engraving and woodcut.

202. *The 'Potence', the collar of the herald 'Golden Fleece', King of Arms of the famous Order of Chivalry. Since 1708 its appearance has not changed, but it must have been originally created after 1517 or at the beginning of the rule of Charles V as King of Spain (Charles I). The collar of heavy gold is decorated with the armorial bearings (in enamel) of former members of the Order and in the centre with the arms (above) and the badge (below) of Charles, as Archduke of Austria and Duke of Burgundy. Kunsthistorisches Museum, Vienna, Austria.*

203. *The arms of the Emperor Charles V in a window (1532) of the old town hall of Regensburg, Bavaria, West Germany, a typical Renaissance design. The imperial eagle is charged on the breast with the arms of Austria and Burgundy ancient (without the red bordure). The shield is encircled by the collar of the Golden Fleece and ensigned with the imperial crown.*

204. *Marble memorial of Eleanor of Aragon (1358–1382) in the chapel de los Reyes Nuevos of the cathedral of Toledo, Spain. The statue of the praying queen was created by Jorge de Contreras in 1534. The gilded relief work, resembling the work of a gold- or silver-smith, is characteristic of the Plateresco. Eleanor was the daughter of Peter IV King of Aragon and his third wife Eleanor of Sicily. She was married to John, King of Castile (1379–1390) in 1375.*

205. *The royal arms, quartered of Castile and Leon, giving an embellishing note to a grille in the chapel de los Reyes Nuevos (from between 1531 and 1534) in the cathedral of Toledo. The dragons are not heraldic supporters but typical ornaments of the plateresque style.*

206. *Woodcarving of the arms of Tirol in the Monastery of St Martin in Gnadenwald, 1558. The chaplet, resting on the shield, became part of the arms in the first third of the eighteenth century, when it was placed behind the head of the eagle. From Das Tiroler Landeswappen.*

207. *Brass monument of Gottfried Wernher Count and Lord of Zimmern, Wildenstein and Messkirch, who died in 1554. At that time shields were not part of a military leader's equipment any more. The effigy is shown without any heraldic embellishment, but the armorial bearings are displayed in the background. Messkirch, Württemberg.*

208. *Frederick III, the Wise, Prince Elector of Saxony, 1463–1525. Copper engraving by Albrecht Dürer, 1524. In the background are the arms of Saxony (right) and the Archmarshal of the Holy Roman Empire. This office was hereditary, but the functions connected to it were delegated to the hereditary Marshals, the Counts zu Pappenheim.*

209. *Portrait of Cardinal Albrecht von Brandenburg, Prince Elector of Mainz, Archbishop of Magdeburg, Administrator of the Bishopric of Halberstadt, 1490–1545. Copper engraving by Albrecht Dürer, 1523. In the background are his arms as a Cardinal. The shield is quartered of Brandenburg, Pomerania, (Burggraf von) Nürnberg and Hohenzollern. The inescutcheons stand for Mainz, the Dukedom of Magdeburg and the Prince-Bishopric of Halberstadt. The sword and the pastoral staff, crossed in saltire behind the shield, symbolize secular and spiritual jurisdiction.*

210. *Bookplate with the canting arms of Johannes Tscherte (*čert *means a devil or savage in the Czech language) by Albrecht Dürer from probably 1518. Tscherte, a friend of Dürer, was architect to the imperial court of Maximilian I.*

211. *The coat of arms of Johann Stabius, historiographer and court astronomer to Emperor Maximilian I. Woodcut by Albrecht Dürer from c.1521. The laurel wreath (above left) symbolizes the poeta laureatus; the design with compasses and tongs (above right) is his personal badge. The archducal crown on the helm, granted by Maximilian, is an extremely unusual honour.*

Bookplates are labels of various sizes, executed as woodcuts, copper engravings, lithographs, drawings and colour prints. They are pasted on the inside cover of a book to identify the owner by displaying his armorial bearings or any other design relating to his person or family.

The bookplate originates from the second half of the fifteenth century, when with the invention of bookprinting (1450) the collecting of books became less expensive. Since such bookplates were mainly used by owners of a library, it became customary to place before their names the Latin words EX LIBRIS, meaning 'from the books of . . .', which is the reason why bookplates also became known as Exlibris.

212. *The armorial achievement of Florian Waldauff, of Hall, Tirol. Woodcut ascribed to Albrecht Dürer, 1517. The shield is encircled by the collar of the Schwanenorden (Brandenburg) and accompanied on the left by the insignia of the Orden de la Jara (Aragon), on the right by an English Collar of Esses.*

213. *A triangular composition of the imperial arms and the two shields of the Free Imperial City of Nürnberg (Nuremberg). Such arrangements appear also since the fifteenth century in Switzerland, when free imperial cities placed two shields of the city next to each other and the imperial arms (sometimes the eagle without shield) above.*

In the case of Nürnberg this looks quite normal, since the city is one of the very few having two coats of arms. In the illustration the grand arms are on the left (the harpy is today an eagle with a king's head) and the small arms on the right. Woodcut by Albrecht Dürer that appeared in the book Die Reformation der Stadt Nürnberg *in 1521.*

Figs. 208 to **213** are from *Klassiker der Kunst*, volume 4 *Dürer*, by Valentin Scherer, Stuttgart and Leipzig, Deutsche Verlags-Anstalt, 1908.

214. *St George and the slain dragon. In the upper left the arms of the Archmarshal of the Holy Roman Empire, the Prince Elector of Saxony.*

215. *Knight as a symbol of nobility. The G on the horse's trapper could possibly stand for St George.*

Figs. 214–215 show woodcuts by Lucas Cranach the elder, 1472–1553. At the beginning of the High Renaissance a revival of the tournament took place. Yet we notice in some illustrations by artists like Dürer, Cranach, Burgkmair and others that the caparisons of the horses do not necessarily bear the arms of a knight any more but are more often decorated with badges, letters and mottoes, or are simply striped in the livery colours. The tilting helm is replaced by a vizored helm, the armet, and heraldic crests are ousted by ostrich plumes, which may also serve as a substitute for mantling. If heraldic shields appear in such pictures they are not part of the knight's equipment but decorate the background.

Figs. 216–221 are woodcuts from *Jost Amman's Wappen- & Stammbuch*, published by Sigmundt Feyrabend in Frankfurt am Main, 1589. New publication in 1923, G. Hirth's Verlag, München, Bavaria, Germany.

216. *The coat of arms of the Duke of Württemberg, quartered of Württemberg, Teck, the 'Reichssturmfahne' (banner of the Empire) and Mömpelgard (Montbéliard).*

217. *The coat of arms of the Lochner family. Woodcuts by Jost Amman, 1539–1591.*

218. *The coat of arms of the Archbishop of Mainz, Prince Elector of the Holy Roman Empire.*

219. *The coat of arms of the family Landschaden von Steinach. Note the unusual mantling.*

220. *The coat of arms of the Fürsten (Princes) von Henneberg (extinct in 1583).*

221. *The coat of arms of the von Reiffenberg family.*

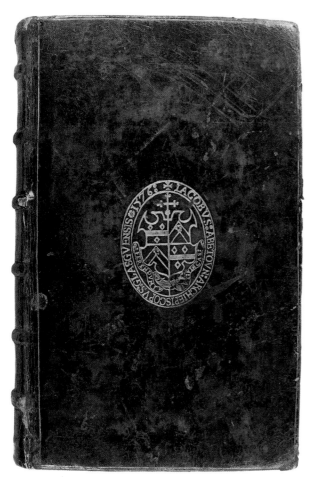

222. *Book bound in calf for James Beaton, Archbishop of Glasgow, 1576. The arms are quarterly 1 and 4, a fess between three mascles (Beaton), 2 and 3, on a chevron an otter's head erased (Balfour), with the archiepiscopal staff behind the shield and the salmon at the foot for the Archdiocese of Glasgow and the motto FERENDUM UT VINCAS ('Endure to succeed'). National Library of Scotland, Edinburgh.*

223. *This book was bound in limp vellum for Mary de Medici (1573–1642), Queen of Henry IV, King of France (1553–1610). After the assassination of the king she became Regent of France. She was the mother of Louis XIII, King of France. The arms of France impaling those of Medici. The topmost roundel of the Medici arms is an augmentation, granted to Piero de Medici by King Louis XI in 1465. National Library of Scotland, Edinburgh.*

Towards the end of the fifteenth century armorial bearings, functioning as marks of property, began to be used on book covers of leather, which are called Super-Libros in some countries. They were impressed or engraved and usually gilded. Such heraldic book-bindings are today still in use for family histories and visitor's books.

SEVENTEENTH CENTURY
✳

224. *Detail of an iron Renaissance key, showing the arms of Saxony impaled with the arms of the Archmarshal of the Holy Roman Empire. The targe (shield à bouche) is ensigned with the hat of a prince elector.*

225. *This key, probably from the first half of the seventeenth century, shows the arms of Saxony, the shield also being ensigned with an electoral hat.*

Figs. 224, 225 and **257** are from *Schönheit von Schloss, Schlüssel, Beschlag,* by D. Prochnow and Rolf Fahrenkrog, A. Henn Verlag, Ratingen, Düsseldorf 1966.

226. *Typical Baroque design of the arms of an abbot with temporal power at the Castle of Schussenried, a former abbey of the Premonstratensian Order, Württemberg, West Germany.*

227. *Book bound in calf for Henry Frederick, Prince of Wales (1594–1612), son of James I (VI), King of the Scots 1567, King of England 1603, and Anne, daughter of Frederick II, King of Denmark. The royal arms of England with a label impressed in silver, and the royal badge of a crowned rose in the corners. National Library of Scotland, Edinburgh.*

228. *Bookplate of probably Alexandre de Cordes, Seigneur de Guisegnies, de la Barre et d'Hourdellies, Lieutenant General of the bailiwicks of Tournai and Tournaisis, died 1650. Copper engraving.*

229. *Bookplate of Guillaume de Halmale, Seigneur de L'Espine, councillor of the Grand Council of Mechlin, Spanish Netherlands in 1664. Copper engraving.*

Figs. 228–230 and **246–248** are bookplates from Benjamin Linnig's *Bibliothèques & Ex-Libris d'amateurs belges aux XVII-XIXmes siècles*, Paris, 1906, and *Quelques Ex-Libris belges anciens*, Paris, 1921; and P. Denis du Peage's *Ex-Libris de Flandres et d'Artois*, Lille, 1934, 2 vols.

230. *Bookplate of Diethelm Scherer, a Swiss officer in the service of Spain, who settled as a merchant in Lille, 1626, and was ennobled by Emperor Ferdinand III in 1646. Copper engraving.*

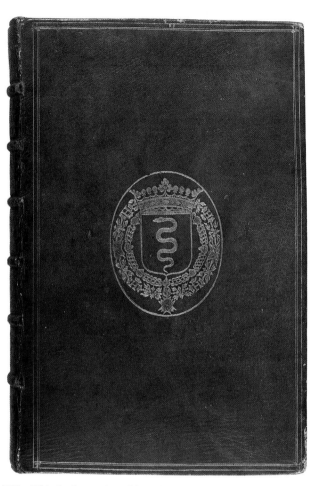

231. *This book was bound in red morocco for Jean-Baptiste Colbert (1619–1683), French Minister of Finances under King Louis XIV. In the centre are his arms encircled by the collars of the Orders of Saint-Michel and Saint-Esprit, and ensigned with the coronet of a French marquis. (Colbert had been created Marquis de Seignelay by his king.) National Library of Scotland, Edinburgh.*

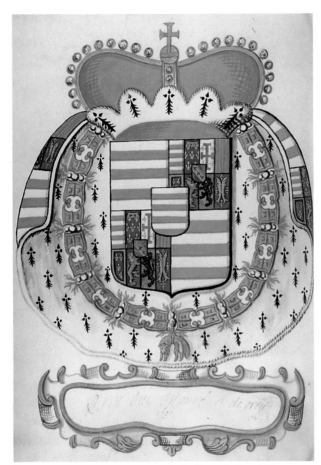

232. *Arms of Ferdinand François de Croÿ, Duke of Havré, Marshal of the Holy Roman Empire, Knight of the Golden Fleece. This painting is from 1691 and shows the arms of the house of Croÿ quartered with the grand arms of Lorraine (because of the marriage of Philip II of Croÿ with Anne of Lorraine, c.1545). The inescutcheon stands for Hungary ancient, since the family was believed (wrongly) to descend from the Arpad dynasty.*

233. *Arms of Anne-Elisabeth of Lorraine-Elbeuf, Princess of Vaudémont. She was one of the ten children of Charles, Duke of Elbeuf (died 1692), and died unmarried in 1714.*

Illustrations from a manuscript (1643–1723) in the City Library of Antwerp, Belgium, *Registre de la confrérie de la Sagrada Passion, etc., a Anvers*, Cod. 45 B.11489, A. Dermul, Catalogue des manuscripts, 1939.

234. *Cabinet d'armes of a member of the family de Schietere, who died in 1637. In the four corners are the arms of his grandparents de Schietere and de la Cuvellerie (father and mother) and de Damhouder and de Chantraines dit Broucxsault (both grandmothers). Church of Our Lady in Bruges, Belgium.*

235. *Cabinet d'armes of Alfonse Anchemant, Seigneur of Beke, who died in 1624, and his wife Anna de la Motte, from 1625. In the centre his wife's arms are surrounded by the cordeliere of a widow. The lozenge is parted per pale of Anchemant and de la Motte (quartered with Catville). His ancestral arms are displayed on the left, his wife's on the right. Church of Our Lady in Bruges, Belgium.*

236. *The book on the left was published in 1627. The cover is embellished with the emblem of the Societas Jesu. The cover of the book in the middle, published in 1606, shows the arms of the Prince Electors of the Rhenish Palatinate. The book on the right was published in 1719. The cover shows the arms of the city of 's Hertogenbosch in Northern Brabant, Netherland. From the Library of the University Faculties St Ignatius at Antwerp [U.F.S.I.A], Belgium.*

237. *Arms of Maximilian II Emmanuel, Prince Elector of Bavaria, some time Stadtholder of the Spanish Netherlands, Knight of the Golden Fleece, 1662–1726.*

238. *The arms of Joachim Ernst, Duke of Holstein-Plön, Knight of the Golden Fleece, died 1671.*

239. *Post office sign from c. 1725, displaying the royal arms of Prussia encircled by the collar of the Order of the Black Eagle. A post horn is suspended from the Baroque cartouche. Bundespostmuseum in Frankfurt am Main, West Germany.*

Figs. **237** and **238** are from the *Registre de la confrérie de la Sagrada Passion.*

EIGHTEENTH CENTURY

240. *Armorial achievement of Don José de Laspiur, Marquis de Villalta, Fieldmaster of the Spanish Infantry, in 1709–1711–1712, died in Brussels in 1715. The arms are adorned with a trophy, an ornamentation representing a group of military weapons, flags, drums, etc.*

241. *Arms of marriage of Georg von Ettenhard, Knight of the Holy Roman Empire, and his wife. From the* Registre de la confrérie de la Sagrada Passion, *etc.*

242. *Epitaph with the portrait in marble relief of Jean Philyppe René d'Yve, Baron d'Ostiche, Vicomte de Bavay, Seigneur de Warelles, Lieutenant General of the Armies of the King (Louis XIV of France), Superintendant of the Gendarmerie of Flanders and Governor of Bruges, married to Dame Marie Madeleine de Béthune du de Splancq. He died in 1706.*

Above the portrait are the arms of d'Yve de Bavay supported by two savages. On the left side the arms of Proissy Bavay, de la Hamïde, Bievres, de Cordes, d'Auxy Warelles, Oyenbrugge, d'Enghien, Béthune; on the right side the arms of Béthune, Cotrel, Havreck, Flechin, Herin, La Fosse, Grault and Hybert. Church of St Salvator in Bruges, Belgium.

243. *This book was bound for Mary d'Este (1658–1718), widow of James II (VII), King of Great Britain (deposed in 1689). She was the daughter of Alphonso IV, Duke of Modena. The arms of Great Britain and Este are surrounded with the cordelière of a widow and ensigned with the royal crown. Around 1500 lacs d'amour (love knots) began to be used in connection with the arms of women. If they appear as parts of a cordelière they generally symbolize widowhood. National Library of Scotland, Edinburgh.*

244. *Funeral hatchment of a member of the famous book printer family Moretus (Moerentorf) from 1757, in the Plantin-Moretus-Museum in Antwerp, Belgium.*

245. *The arms of Humbertus Guilielmus de Precipiano, Archbishop of Mechlin (1689–1711), Primate of the Spanish Netherlands. From the* Registre de la confrérie de la Sagrada Passion, *etc.*

247. *Bookplate of Melchior-Joseph de Villegas, Baron d'Hovorst, Seigneur de Vierzel, Bouchout, Werster, etc, a descendant of a Spanish nobleman at the court of Emperor Charles V. In 1736 he became Receiver General of the domains of Emperor Charles VI in Mechlin and Antwerp and died in 1761. Copper engraving by F. Harrewyn.*

246. *The arms of Guillaume-Albert de Grysperre, Baron de Goick et de Libersart, 1638–1725, President and Chancellor of the Grand Council of Brabant. Two silver-gilt maces, symbols of his office, are crossed in saltire behind the shield, which is ensigned with the bonnet of a baron brabançon. Copper engraving by J. Berterham.*

248. *Bookplate of Liduine-Marie-Agnes van der Nath, Abbess of Roosendael near Mechlin, died in1742, or of her sister Isabelle van der Nath, Abbess of Nazareth near Lierre, 1689–1767, daughters of Jacques-Louis van der Nath, Count of the Holy Roman Empire. Behind the shield the crozier of an abbess with sudarium. Copper engraving by F. Diamaer.*

249. *The castle in Würzburg, Bavaria, West Germany, was built between 1719 and 1744 in a mixture of Italian and French Baroque by Johann Balthasar Neumann, 1687–1753, for the Prince Bishop Johann Philipp von Schönborn. The arms of the prince bishop, ensigned with the hat of a prince and supported by two lions, are displayed below the imperial crown.*

250. *The coat of arms of the von Kummer family, granted by Frederick William II, King of Prussia, is taken from the letters patent by which Hans Wilhelm Kummer was raised to hereditary nobiliary status in 1786.*

251 and **252.** *Two post office signs from the Principality of Hesse-Cassel, the one on the left from about 1750, the one on the right from 1763. The informally-balanced frames of the cartouches are characteristic of the Rococo. Bundespostmuseum in Frankfurt am Main.*

NINETEENTH CENTURY

*

253. *Book bound in purple morocco tooled in blind and gold for David Constable (1795–1867) the son of Sir Walter Scott's publisher. The arms are quarterly gules and vair, overall a bend Or, with the crest of a greyhound passant and the motto IMPIGER ET FIDUS ('Indefatigable and true'). National Library of Scotland, Edinburgh.*

254. *The arms of Nicholas Rolin, Knight, Citizen of Autun, Seigneur of Authume, Chancellor of Burgundy, and his second wife Guigone de Salins. In 1443 they founded the famed Hôtel-Dieu in Beaune (today in the Arrondissement Côte-d'or, France). The glass is part of a restoration of the Chapel of the great Ward in the hospital, carried out in the nineteenth century.*

255. *Window in the Cathedral of Our Lady of Antwerp, Belgium. The scene in the centre, Alexander Farnese presenting the key to the city, is surrounded by the armorial bearings of families and persons who played an important role in the turbulent history of Antwerp during the sixteenth century. The third coat of arms on the left, from the bottom up, for instance, is the one of Count Egmont, the papal arms in the centre above belong to Sixtus V. The window is the work of Stalins and Janssens, 1884.*

256. *The regalia and crowns of imperial Russia. Original drawing of this still life by A. Zemtsova,* gravure by *M. Rashevski,* from Coronation in Moscow, *a special issue of the Russian periodical Niva, No. 21, 1883. This picture shows applied heraldry all over. The collar of the Order of St Andrew is partly composed of Russian double-headed eagles, which appear on other objects as well, even on the blade of the sword.*

257. *Detail of a ceremonial key of gilded bronze for a chamberlain at the court of the King of Bavaria. The royal arms are displayed on a pavilion and surrounded by the collars of the four highest Bavarian orders. From Schönheit von Schloss, Schlüssell Beschlag.*

258. *Seal with the grand arms of imperial Russia, as used on the credentials of members of the diplomatic corps under the Czars Alexander III and Nicholas II. From the author's collection.*

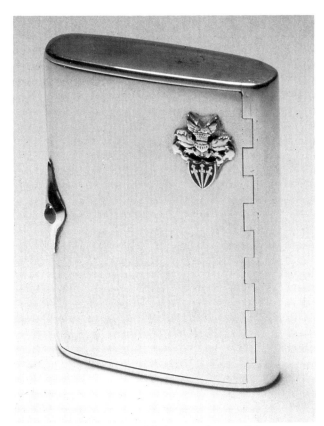

259. *Silver cigarette case with the coat of arms of the von Volborth family of St Petersburg, Russia, c.1900. The shield is of red enamel. Actual length 9.5 cm.*

260. *Crystal glass engraved with the coat of arms of the German family von Keudell, from the end of the nineteenth century, 27.7 cm high.*

TWENTIETH CENTURY

———— * ————

261. *Silver cup engraved with the coat of arms of the von Volborth family. German, 1941. Actual height 7.5 cm.*

По указу
ЕГО ВЕЛИЧЕСТВА ГОСУДАРЯ ИМПЕРАТОРА
НИКОЛАЯ АЛЕКСАНДРОВИЧА
САМОДЕРЖЦА ВСЕРОССІЙСКАГО,
и прочая, и прочая, и прочая

262. *Official version of the double-headed eagle of the Empire of Russia, from the engraving on a diplomatic passport of 1910.*

263. *The double-headed eagle of the Empire of Russia enlarged. The arms of Moscow in the centre. The arms of Kazan, Poland, Taurida and Kiev (with Novgorod and Vladimir) are on the dexter wing, the arms of Astrakhan, Siberia, Georgia and Finland on the sinister. The arms in the centre are surrounded by the collar of the Order of St. Andrew.*

264. *The royal arms of Netherland, painted by J.E. van Leeuwen for the High Council of the Nobility in The Hague, 1907. In the official blazon the pavilion is described as of purple colour. Nowadays, however, it is usually painted red.*

265. *The royal arms of the Netherlands as displayed on the sign of the Consulat General in Antwerp, Belgium.*

266. *Memorial for the one million dead of the British Empire who fell in the Great War 1914–1918, many of whom rest in Belgium. Cathedral of Our Lady of Antwerp, Belgium. In the middle of the heraldic composition are the royal arms of Great Britain and Ireland, surrounded by the arms of India, Canada, South Africa, New Zealand, Newfoundland and Australia.*

267. *The arms of the Barons de Rothschild carved over the entrance of the Château de La Muette in Paris, France. The house was built for the family in the classical style of the eighteenth century and completed in 1922. It is now headquarters of the Organization for Economic Co-operation and Development.*

HERALDRY HAS NEVER completely disappeared from military life and its traces can still be found on military uniforms, flags and equipment.

268. *Prussian infantry helm ('Pickelhaube') from World War I, adorned with the Prussian eagle, bearing the motto (from wing to wing): Mit Gott für König und Vaterland, i.e. 'With God for King and Country'.*

269. *Cap badge of an officer of the United States Navy. In contrast to the arms of the USA, the clouds and stars around the eagle's head are removed. The stars are placed in the chief of the shield.*

270. *A crane in its vigilance in the arms of the Situation Center, a department of NATO. Original design by the author, 1983. Metal work by Frank Claes.*

271. *The small arms of the Empire of Russia as used on army fur hats, c.1900.*

272. *The arms of the Kingdom of Belgium as used on caps and tropical helmets by administrative and judicial functionaries and also by officers of the 'Force Publique' of the Belgian Congo (now Zaïre) before 1960.*

273. *The Royal Arms as used in Scotland, carved on the front of the Sovereign's stall in the Chapel of the Thistle in the Church of St Giles, Edinburgh, Scotland. The chapel was built in 1911. The Royal Arms were designed by John Sutherland, carved (and possibly tinted) by the Clow brothers who were responsible for carving all the woodwork in the chapel.*

274. *The armorial achievement of Ronald Ruthven, 11th Earl of Leven and 10th Earl of Melville, Knight of the Order of the Thistle, 1835–1906. Stone relief outside the Chapel of the Thistle. The architectural setting was designed by Sir Robert Lorimer, the architect of the present chapel. The heraldic drawing for the stone carver was prepared by John Sutherland, who was a teacher at the Edinburgh College of Art.*

275. *The coat of arms of Franz Seraph Hye Edler von Kerkdal. Painted woodcarving by Hans Gänzer, Ampass, Innsbruck, Austria, 1979.*

276. *Arms of marriage of Hervé Douxchamps and his wife Josiane, née de Wouters d'Oplinter-Bouchout. Carved in stone, 25 × 30 cm, by Andres Ponteville, Brussels, Belgium. Second half of the twentieth century.*

PART III

---✳---

PART III

───── ✳ ─────

AN INTERNATIONAL EXHIBITION OF HERALDIC WORKS BY ARTISTS & ARTISANS FROM THE END OF THE NINETEENTH CENTURY TILL TODAY

───── ✳ ─────

INTRODUCTION
———— ✳ ————

IN SPITE OF the fact that heraldry is bound by ancient rules and customs to certain traditional forms, the artist is allowed to have a very individualistic style of his own. He may also be influenced by one or the other past or contemporary approach to design and its expressivity, yet he is not supposed to break through the boundaries of what could be called an heraldic style, meaning a distinct expression of the heraldic spirit, as we know it from the Gothic and the early Renaissance.

After a long period of slow decay, the medievalism of the Romantic era had fanned the interest in heraldry back into life. But it was not before the last decades of the nineteenth century that this new interest began to find adequate artistic expression.

I always regretted that it was so difficult to get acquainted with the work of heraldic artists, their personal approach, their techniques and the influence that the cultural environment in their countries might have on their style. But to enjoy their creativity, to compare and evaluate their talents and standards, it would take heraldic exhibitions; yet they are extremely rare and in addition not necessarily arranged by artistic motivation. Thus the plan ripened to collect material for such an exhibition in this book. I knew a few contemporary artists, but I needed more. They were not easy to find, especially in foreign countries. Most of them graciously responded to my invitation to take part in this show and sent me examples of their work in photographs or transparencies. Originals unfortunately were not always available for the printing, which is the reason why some of the reproductions cannot live up to the quality of the originals, especially of very delicate and intricate work in colour. Nevertheless, I believe that from the following pages the reader can get a small and fragmentary outlook on the variety of heraldic art in the past hundred years. I hope that the range of this exhibition is wide enough to interest and please the connoisseur, to stimulate the student of heraldic art and to be an aid to the layman who wants to distinguish better between artistic, routinized and amateurish work.

JOÃO PAULO de ABREU e LIMA, 1922
(Lisbon, Portugal)

277. *Bookplate of Martim Eduardo Côrte-Real de Albuquerque. India ink drawing, 1969. The M in the small canton in dexter chief is a mark of difference.*

278. *The coat of arms of the family Guedes Vaz Costa Carvalho. Illuminated parchment, 1979.*

279. *The artist's own coat of arms (Abreu Rocha Oliveira Lima). Illuminated parchment, 1979.*

280. *Bookplate of Manuel José de Ferreira Pinto Leão, India ink drawing, 1967.*

281. *Bookplate of the Marquesses de Sabugosa, Counts of São Lourenco, India ink drawing, 1963.*

282. *Bookplate of Dr José Augusto Fragozo Fernandes, India ink drawing, 1961.*

284. *Detail of a Portuguese grant of a coat of arms and a banner to the Corporation of Sciences, Arts and Letters. 1966, illuminated parchment. The corporations were abolished after 1974.*

283. *Detail of a Portuguese grant of a coat of arms and a banner to the Corporation of Sports and Physical Education. 1966, illuminated parchment.*

285. *Detail of a Portuguese grant of a coat of arms and a banner to the Corporation of Assistance (social services), 1966, illuminated parchment.*

287. *Super-Libros, India ink drawing, 1970. The armorial bearings of the Count of Albuquerque.*

286. *The armorial bearings of Portugal, a proposition to return to the traditional line; the actual arms of the present republic consist of the shield only, placed upon an armillary sphere. India ink, 1963. The shield is encircled by the collar of the Order of the Tower and the Sword and supported by two angels, charged on the breast with the plaque of the Three Orders, of Christ, of Avis and of Sant'Iago, and holding banners with the cross of the Order of Christ (left) and the armillary sphere (right), which has been used for centuries as the badge of Portugal. The motto is PELA LEI E PELA GREI ('By the law, by the people'), the war cry 'S. Jorge' (St George).*

288. *Bookplate of Augusto d'Athayde, China ink drawing, 1983. The badges of a Commander of the Order of Christ and a Knight of Honour and Devotion of the Order of Malta are suspended from the shield.*

ZDENKO G. ALEXY, 1922 (Bratislava, Czechoslovakia)

289. *Bookplate, 1982, designed for Sir Alexander Colin Cole, Garter Principal King of Arms. The shields of Garter and Cole ancient are encircled by a collar of Esses and ensigned with the coronet of an English king of arms. Two Garter sceptres are crossed in saltire behind the shields.*

EX LIBRIS

CYRILLI DUDÁŠ

290. *Bookplate of Dr Cyril Dudáš, Canon, Collegiate Chapter of St Martin, Bratislava. The decoration on a green ribbon was conferred to the Chapter in perpetuo by Emperor Francis I of Austria.*

EX LIBRIS

DOUCE & JEAN-CLAUDE LOUTSCH

291. *Bookplate of Dr Jean-Claude Loutsch and his wife Douce, nee Weydert, Luxemburg.*

KAREN BAILEY, 1960 (Ottawa, Ontario, Canada)

292. *Maximilian ('. . . the paths of glory lead but to the grave').*

293. *Design of a Wyvern.*

294. *Small hatchment with the arms of Rita H. Le Couteur, 1873–1956, of St Helier's, Jersey, Channel Isles. St James' Anglican Church, Paris, Ontario, Canada.*

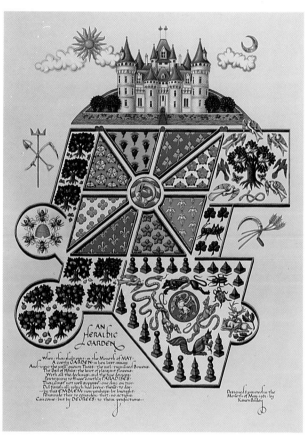

295. *An heraldic garden ('. . . no actions can come, but by degrees, to their perfections').*

296. *An heraldic map showing the armorial bearings of Canada and the provinces.*

297. *Central Medallion design for Mayor's Chain of Office for North Vancouver, British Columbia, Canada.*

SIR ALEXANDER COLIN COLE, Garter King of Arms, 1922 (London, England)

298. *Drawing of his own arms (Cole, modern) ensigned with the coronet of an English King of Arms.*

PATRICIA BERTRAM, 1927 (Herald Painter at the Court of the Lord Lyon, Edinburgh, Scotland)

299. *The arms of Malcom Rognvald Innes of Edingight, Baron of Yeochrie CVO, KStJ, WS, FSA Scot, as Marchmont Herald of Arms, before he became Lord Lyon King of Arms; parted per pale of the arms of his Office as Lyon Clerk and Keeper of the Records, and of Innes of Edingight. The shield is surrounded by a Collar of Esses, from which his badge of office is suspended, and ensigned with the chapeau of a Scottish territorial baron.*

HENRY GRAY (Herald Painter at the College of Arms, London, England)

300. *The arms of Sir Alexander Colin Cole, KCVO, TD, OStJ, FSA, Garter Principal King of Arms, with decorations and the insignia of his office of Garter Principal King of Arms, and accompanied on the left by the arms of the office of Garter, on the right by the shield of the College of Arms.*

HANS DIETRICH BIRK, 1916
(Scarborough, Ontario, Canada)

The armorial bearings in this section (**Figs. 301–318**) belong to noble families of Europe, which came as immigrants into Canada. They are from the *Canadian Ethnic Armorial*, deposited at The National Archives in Ottawa. Collected and painted by the artist, and published in 1983 as *Armorial Heritage* in Canada.

301. *von Boch-Galhau, of French origin, Prussian nobility.*

302. *von Wühlisch, of German origin.*

303. *Ignatiev, of Russian origin.*

304. *Zurowski (arms Leliwa), of Polish origin.*

305. *von Schroeter, of German origin.*

306. *Giannelia von Philergos, Austrian nobility.*

307. *von Fircks, of Baltic origin.*

308. *von Hardenberg, of German origin.*

309. *von Pfetten, of German origin.*

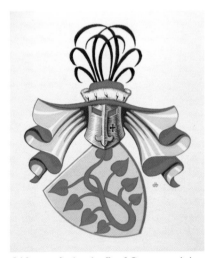

310. *von Seckendorff, of German origin.*

311. *von Reuss, of German origin.*

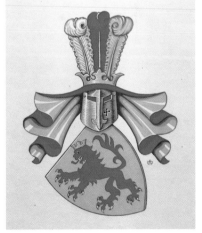

312. *von Unruh, of German origin.*

313. *von Merveldt, of German origin.*

314. *von Schaesberg, of German origin.*

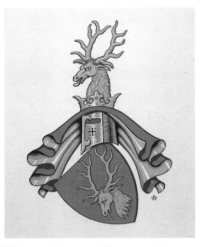

315. *von Trampe, of German origin.*

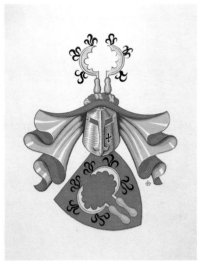

316. *von Lüttichau, of German origin.*

317. *von Imhoff, of German origin.*

318. *von Bistram (arms Tarnawa), of Polish origin.*

JAIME BUGALLAL Y VELA, 1937
(La Rochelle, France)

The arms of a Spanish Grandee (**Fig. 319**) and the arms of a Spanish Count (**Fig. 321**) have been published in the *Gran Enciclopedia Gallega*.

319. *The arms of Don Gonzalo Ozores, Seigneur de la Casa de Rubianes, Marquis d'Aranda, a Grandee of Spain. The arms are quartered of Caamaño (Casa de Rubianes) and Aranda. The inescutcheon bears the arms of Ozores.*

320. *The coat of arms of Don Eduardo Pardo de Guevara, olim de Saavedra, is quartered of Pardo (in Galicia) and Ribadeneira. The inescutcheon bears the arms of Saavedra.*

321. *The arms of Don José Ramón F. Bugallal y Barrón, Count de Bugallal.*

156

CHARLES JOHN BURNETT, Dingwall Pursuivant of Arms, 1940 (Edinburgh, Scotland)

322. *Armorial achievement of Martin M. Cruikshank of Anchreoch, Knight of Justice of the venerable Order of St John of Jerusalem. The red cap of maintenance and robe of estate show the armiger is a Scottish territorial baron in possession of his barony. In the British Order of St John members from the rank of a Knight of Grace on may place the simple Cross of the Order behind the shield. In the Order of Malta and the Johanniterorden this is done only by Knight Commanders and higher ranks.*

323. *Panel bearing the coat of arms of King James V of Scotland. The Scottish Sovereign was elected a Knight of the Order of the Golden Fleece at the 20th Chapter of the Order held in Tournai Cathedral (Doornik, Belgium) in 1531. The original panel bearing the King's arms was destroyed during the following centuries. In 1980 the Heraldry Society of Scotland undertook to present a replacement panel to the Cathedral Chapter at Tournai. This the society did at a solemn ceremony held in the cathedral during May 1982.*

The arms were painted by Charles John Burnett, and the lettering is the work of John Curry. The panel is modelled on contemporary sixteenth-century examples and the arms are based on a version which appears in a Scottish Armorial of 1542.

Woodcarvings by COLIN CAMPBELL, 1912 (Belmont, Massachusetts, USA)

324. *The arms of the Committee on Heraldry of the New England Historic Genealogical Society, Boston, Massachusetts, USA.*

325. *The coat of arms of the ancient Dukes of Brabant.*

326. *The arms of Harold Bowditch, M.D., of Brookline, Massachusetts, USA.*

327. *The coat of arms of Major General D.R.D. Fisher, Scotland.*

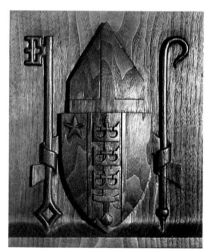

328. *The arms of the Episcopal (Anglican) Diocese of Massachusetts, USA.*

GUSTAV ADOLF CLOSS, 1864–1938 (Germany)

Gustav Adolf Closs was a German painter and heraldist. The illustrations (**Figs. 329–332**) appeared in *Deutscher Wappenkalender* 1939, Deutsche Baumeister (German architects), C.A. Starke Verlag, Görlitz, Silesia.

329. *Coat of arms of the German family von Klenze, Bavarian nobility, 1833.*

330. *Coat of arms of the German family Spitta, originating in the sixteenth century from Verviers (Belgium).*

331. *Coat of arms of the German family von Knobelsdorff, noblesse de race (Meissen, thirteenth century).*

332. *Coat of arms of the German family von Erdmannsdorf, Saxon noblesse de race (Meissen, thirteenth century).*

DANIEL de BRUIN, 1950
(Krimpen aan den Ijssel, Netherland)

333. *Bookplate of Walther Ballerstedt, Buch, West Germany. India ink drawing, 1982.*

334. *Bookplate of Dr Peter Nawroth, Hamburg, West Germany. India ink drawing, 1984.*

335. *Bookplate of Dom Bernard Daeleman, O.S.B., Dendermonde, Belgium. India ink drawing, 1983.*

336. *Bookplate of Willem F. De Kovel, Rotterdam, Netherland. India ink drawing, 1981.*

337. *Bookplate of Albert Luyendijk, Vlissingen, Netherland. India ink drawing, 1982.*

338. *Bookplate of Rinus Schot, Breda, Netherland. India ink drawing, 1981.*

RENÉ de CRAMER, (Ghent, Belgium)

Figs. 339–345 are from *Drapeaux, Bannières, Souvenir de la Vieille Flandre*, a catalogue of the World Exhibition of Ghent, 1913.

339. *The Draper's Hall of Ypres, West Flanders, with the arms of Flanders and Ypres.*

340. *The Belfry of Ghent, East Flanders, with the arms of Flanders (left) and Ghent.*

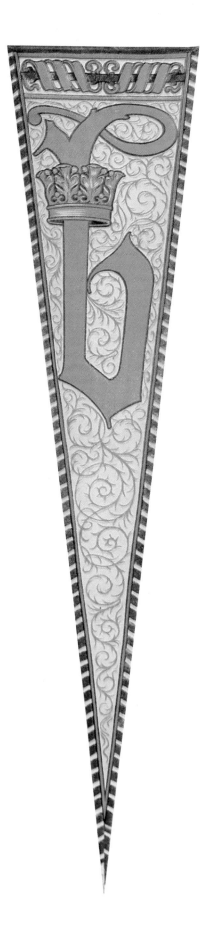

341. *Pennon with the badge of Bruges, West Flanders.*

342. *The arms of Nieuwpoort, a town in West Flanders.*

343. *The coat of arms of Messire van Vilsteren, Seigneur de Laerne.*

344. *The coat of arms of Messire de Schoutheete, Seigneur de Laerne.*

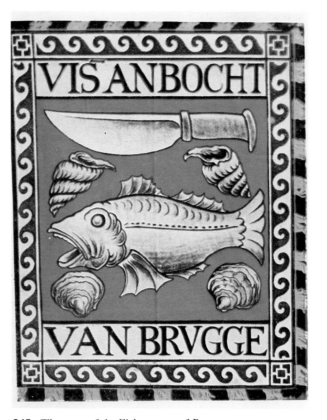

345. *The arms of the Fishmongers of Bruges.*

EMIL DOEPLER, THE YOUNGER, 1855–1922
(Germany)

346. *This armorial super-achievement, drawn with outstanding craftsmanship, looks like a monument of the prosperous last decades of the nineteenth century. It is composed of the arms of the heraldic society Der Herold in Berlin and of members thereof, showing all the possible appurtenances of a grand achievement in German heraldry. The supporters hold banners of Berlin and the heraldic tent is topped by a banner of the German Empire. Drawing from F. Warnecke's* Heraldisches Handbuch [Manual of Heraldry], *published by C.A. Starke, Görlitz, Silesia, in 1880 and reprinted by C.A. Starke Verlag, Limburg an der Lahn, West Germany, in 1971.*

347. *Cover design for a book by Georg Schuster, which was published by August Scherl G.m.b.H. in Berlin, as a memorial of the Hohenzollern family's 500 years of rule, first as Margraves and Prince Electors of Brandenburg, then as Kings of Prussia and finally as German Emperors. In the centre above are the ancient arms of the family accompanied on the left by its helm and crest and on the right by the arms of Brandenburg, ensigned with a prince elector's hat; below, on the left, are the arms of Prussia, ensigned with the royal crown, and on the right the arms of the German Empire (1871–1918), ensigned with the imperial crown.*

348. *The small imperial arms of Austria. At the turn of the century heraldic art in Germany was influenced by the Renaissance rather than by the Gothic style (from* Heraldisches Handbuch).

349. *The Bavarian coat of arms designed in the style of the early sixteenth century (from* Heraldisches Handbuch).

MANSUETO (called ENNIO) DURANTE, 1917–1982 (Bolzano, Italy)

Figs. 350–352 are From the *Liber Amicorum* of Dr Ladislao de Lászlocky, Bolzano.

CAV. GR. CR. D'OBBEDIENZA
ANTONIO CARLOTTI
MARCHESE DI RIPARBELLA

350. *(Left) The coat of arms of Marchese Antonio Carlotti di Riparbella, Knight Grand Cross of Obedience of the Order of Malta, Delegate for Verona (with Vicenza, Trento, Bolzano), 1904–1983. 1979. The coronet of rank is not the normal one for an Italian marchese but tolerated in Italian heraldry.*

351. *(Right) The coat of arms of Graf Franz Josef Forni (family from Modena), seigneur and land-owner in Tirol, Knight of the Golden Fleece (Austrian branch). 1978. The type of coronet of rank for an Italian count is not the normal one but tolerated in Italian heraldry.*

Franz Graf   Josef Forni

352. *The emblem of the International Academy of Heraldry surrounded by the arms of the members of the Bureau. A memento of the General Assembly of Copenhagen in 1980. The fourteen shields of the outer circle belong to the councillors, the other five to the Secretary General, the 1st Vice-President, the President, the second Vice-President and the Treasurer.*

DAN ESCOTT, 1928 (Avalon, NSW, Australia)

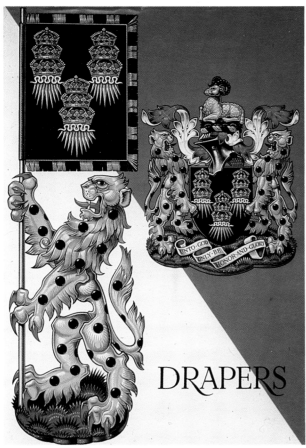

353. *Coat of arms and banner of the Worshipful Company of Drapers of the City of London, granted in 1613 to replace two earlier grants (from 1439 and 1561).*

354. *Coat of arms, banner and badges of John of Lancaster, Duke of Bedford, Knight of the Garter, 1389–1435. He was the third son of Henry IV, King of England, and of Mary de Bohun. The banner shows his arms of marriage to Ann, daughter of John, Duke of Burgundy.*

EDUARDO ESPERANCA (Braga, Portugal)

355. *Armorial bearings of the Portuguese Air Force (F.A.P.).*

356. *Design of armorial bearings for the Base Aerea Nr. 5 which won the first prize in a national competition, 1980.*

357. *This design of armorial bearings for the Portuguese Parachutists won the 1st prize in a national competition.*

358. *Coat of arms of Jose Rosa Aranjo, a Portuguese ethnographer.*

359. *Coat of arms of João Lencastre da Mota, a Portuguese diplomat.*

360. *Coat of arms of Robert Frederick Illing, Consul of the United States in Oporto.*

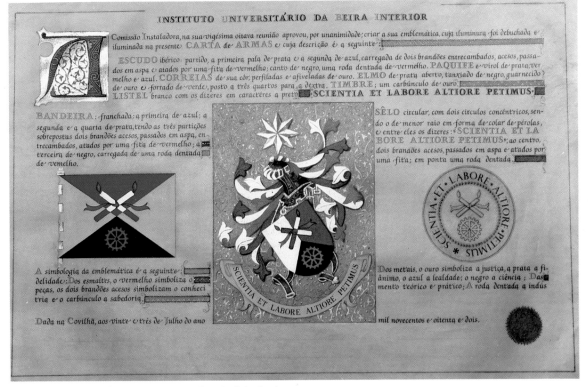

361. *Banner, coat of arms and embossed seal of the Instituto Universitario da Beira Interior in Covilha, 1982.*

IAN GRANT, 1941 (Engraver and Silversmith, Edinburgh, Scotland)

362. *Silver pocket watch, engraved with the arms of Charles John Burnett, of Edinburgh.*

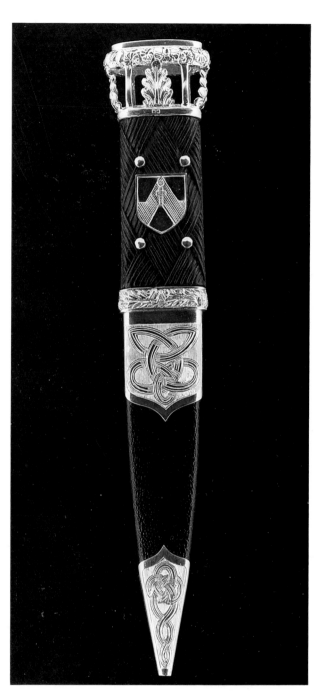

363. *Skean dhu with the arms of John Malden, Scotland, on the hilt. Actual height: 27 cm.*

364. *Belt buckle with crest and motto of Carey Randall, Scotland. Actual size: 11 × 8 cm.*

365. *Cap badge of John Randall, of London. The feather means that he is a Duine Uasail, an armigerous clansman who is not head of a distinct branch of the clan. 12 cm high, silver.*

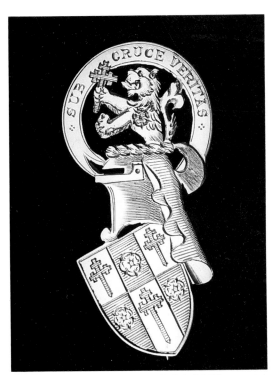

366. *The coat of arms of William Ralph McClymont Adams, of Edinburgh. 5 cm high, silver.*

367. *Silver badge of the chairman of the Heraldry Society of Scotland, showing the arms and the motto of the society meaning 'be aware of heraldry'.*

368. *Pewter mug with the arms of the Heraldry Society of Scotland. 9.5 cm high.*

369. *Silver medal with the arms of John Ramsay Grant, of Edinburgh. Actual size in diameter: 3.5 cm.*

370. *The arms of Mrs Kathleen Stewart, Aberdeenshire, Scotland. The silver brooch is 5 cm high.*

MANDA HANSON, 1960
(Buckhurst Hill, Essex, England)

371. *Badge and banner of the de Bohun, Earls of Hereford. The white swan, ducally gorged and chained, was the badge of the de Bohun and was derived therefrom by Henry V, King of England, 1413–1422. The banner bears the arms of de Bohun: Azure a bend argent, cotised and between six lioncels Or. Scraper-board, 1982.*

372. *The capital letter for Queen Elizabeth II is part of a design for the heading of a royal warrant. Painted on vellum, 1983.*

ROGER HARMIGNIES, 1922 (Brussels, Belgium)

373. *The coat of arms of Hervé Douxchamps, Brussels.*

374. *The coat of arms of Roger Harmignies. Normally the tilting helm is not used in Belgian heraldry but the artist preferred it for aesthetic reasons.*

375. *The arms of the Marquis di Torrebermeja (Lima, Peru).*

376. *Fernand Baron de Ryckman de Betz, 1871–1961.*

377. *The arms of the Viscounts de Ghellinck-Vaernewyck.*

378. *Count Joseph de Borchgrave d'Altena, 1895–1975. The ancient crown of a German count and the manteau were probably granted with the title Count of the Holy Roman Empire by Maximilian- Joseph, Prince Elector of Bavaria and Vicar of the Holy Roman Empire, in 1745.*

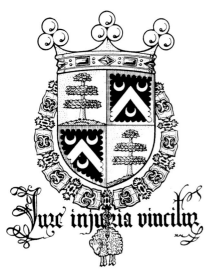

379. *Charles Viscount Terlinden, Knight of the Golden Fleece, 1878–1972.*

380. *Count Pierre de Lichtervelde, Knight of Honour and Devotion of the Sovereign Military Order of Malta, 1884–1954.*

381. *Count Thierry de Limburg Stirum, Knight of the Golden Fleece, 1904–1968. The arms are placed on a manteau with the crown of the formerly ruling counts of the Holy Roman Empire.*

Figs. 377–381 are of the armorial bearings of co-founders of the Office Généalogique et Héraldique de Belgique which appeared in an *Heraldic Calendar 1972*, published by this association.

BRUNO BERNARD HEIM, 1911
(London, England)

382. *The arms of Archbishop Bruno Bernard Heim, a slightly modified version of his Swiss family arms in which the lion holds a blue horseshoe between its forepaws. The lion should normally be turned to dexter.*

383. *The armorial bearings of Theobald David Mathew, Windsor Herald; on the left his badge of office under the royal crown. Beneath that a rebus for Leslie C. Hayward. The emblems chosen are puns on the name: HAY – fork; and the WARD of a key. Both are set in a book which is an allusion to the bearer's profession as publisher.*

384. *The arms of the Count and Prince Emanuel de La Rochefoucald-Montbel.*

Figs. 383–387 and **389** are from Archbishop Heim's *Liber Amicorum et Illustrium Hospitum*, published as *Armorial Bruno B. Heim* by van Duren, Gerrards Cross, England, 1981.

Fig. 388 appeared in *Heraldry in the Catholic Church*, by Bernard Bruno Heim, Van Duren Publishers, Gerrards Cross, 1981.

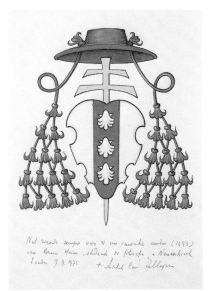

385. *The arms of Michele Cardinal Pellegrino, Archbishop of Turin, Italy.*

386. *The armorial bearings of H.M. Queen Elizabeth, the Queen Mother. (United Kingdom and Northern Ireland impaling quarterley Lyon and Bowes.) The royal supporters were omitted because of lack of space.*

387. *The coat of arms of Hubert Chesshyre and the badge of his office as Chester Herald and a rebus, designed by Sir A. Colin Cole, Garter King of Arms, and painted by B.B. Heim for Graham Beck, Bursar at the College of Arms, showing emblemché an eye surveying and a fountain symbolising flowing water and being a pun on the name Beck.*

388. *The arms of Fra Angelo de Mojana di Cologna, Prince Grand Master of the Sovereign Military Order of Malta. Since he is a professed knight with religious vows, a rosary encircles the shield.*

389. *The arms of Messire Cholet de la Choletiere Marquis Maximo Sciolette, Knight of the Order of the Golden Fleece.*

CON ESTA SEÑAL VENCERAS
390. *The city arms of Puerto de la Cruz, Tenerife, Canary Islands, Spain.*

OTTO HUPP, 1859–1949 (German heraldist)

391. *The coat of arms of the German family von Beneckendorff und Hindenburg as designed for the German field marshal (World War I) Paul von Hindenburg, 1847–1934, who was later President of Germany (1925–1934). From* Münchener Kalender, *1916, G.J. Manz AG, Munich – Regensburg.*

Figs. 393 and**395** are from *Die Wappen und Siegel der Deutschen Städte, Flecken und Dörfer.*

392. *The coat of arms of the German Johann Gensfleisch, called Gutenberg, 1400?–1468, the inventor of printing from movable type.*

394. *The eagle of the German Empire, charged with the shield of the Kingdom of Prussia, bearing on an inescutcheon the arms of the imperial family (Hohenzollern). The shield is encircled by the collar of the Order of the Black Eagle. From* Münchener Kalender, *1916, published by G.J. Manz Akt. Ges., München-Regensburg.*

393. *The arms of Bavaria, chosen in 1923, were quartered of Bavaria, Palatinate, Hohenstaufen and Franconia. The decorative coronet of the republic was called Volkskrone, which means 'crown of the people'.*

395. *The coat of arms of the Count Palatine bei Rhein, Duke in Bavaria, Prince Elector and Vicar of the Holy Roman Empire. The inescutcheon was red and was the symbol of the Office of Vicar of the Empire.*

ANDREW STEWART JAMIESON, 1961
(Sherborne, Dorset, England)

396. *The coat of arms of the Kretschmer family, printers and publishers in Limburg an der Lahn, Hesse, West Germany.*

397. *The coat of arms of Henry le Despencer, Bishop of Norwich.*

398. *The coat of arms of Aquascutum of London, painted at their New York store as a demonstration of heraldic art in 1984.*

ADOLF F.J. KARLOVSKÝ, 1922
(Birsfelden [Basel], Switzerland)

399. *The coat of arms of the family of the world-famous orchestra conductor Herbert Ritter (knight) von Karajan.*

400. *The coat of arms of the ancient Slovakian family Jessenius de Magna Jessen, of which the great physician Johann Jessenius was a member. He was one of the leaders of the revolt of the Bohemian estates against emperor Ferdinand II; and was executed in 1621.*

401. *The coat of arms of the family of Emil Ritter (knight) von Škoda, founder of the machine- and arms-factory Škoda in Pilsen, Bohemia, Czechoslovakia.*

Figs. 399–401 appeared in *Ärzte-und Apotheker-Wappen*, No. 6, by Prof. Dr S. Gutmann, published by W. Spitzner, pharmaceutical works, Ettlingen/Baden, West Germany.

402. *The coat of arms of the Austrian family Edle (nobles) von Hovorka.*

403. *The coat of arms of Kašpar Zdenko Graf (Count) Kaplíerz, Freiherr (Baron) von Sulewicz (1611–1686), imperial Fieldmarshal, President of the Imperial War Council. Two marshal's batons are crossed in saltire behind the shield.*

404. *The arms of a daughter of the Austrian family of Mäderer von Ehrenreichscron.*

405. *The coat of arms of the Austrian Freiherr (Baron) Robert von Procházka.*

JEAN-CLAUDE LOUTSCH, 1932 (Luxembourg)

406. *The armorial bearings of Emperor Charles V. This design, inspired by different seals of the emperor, presents a synthesis of the heraldic symbolism relating to this sovereign. The shield, ensigned by an open royal crown, is placed on the two-headed eagle of the Holy Roman Empire, above which the imperial crown is hovering. The Burgundian badge, the two ragged staves crossed in saltire, shows behind the eagle's heads.*

The eagle is grasping with its claws the crowned Columns of Hercules. To avoid overcrowding of the design, the Order of the Golden Fleece is simply indicated by its badge, steel and flint striking fire.

407. *The armorial bearings of Emperor Charles VI, from his grand seal. The shield, ensigned with a royal crown and encircled by the collar of the Order of the Golden Fleece, is placed on the imperial eagle, holding sceptre, sword and globe. Above is the imperial crown.*

Figs. 406 and **407** are from *Armorial du Pays de Luxembourg*, by Dr Jean-Claude Loutsch, 1974, Ministère des Arts et des Sciences.

R. GORDON M. MACPHERSON, 1926
Burlington, Ontario, Canada)

408. *Bookplate.*

409. *Bookplate.*

410. *Bookplate.*

411. *Bookplate.*

412. *Bookplate.*

413. *Bookplate.*

414. *Bookplate.*

415. *Bookplate.*

416. *Bookplate.*

417. *Bookplate.*

418. *Bookplate.*

419. *Bookplate.*

420. *Bookplate.*

421. *Bookplate.*

RAYMOND MORRIS of Eddergoll, 1930
(Master Leather Carver, Cupar, Fife, Scotland)

422. *The arms of Arnold von Brienz, a knight of the ancient Order of St Lazarus, who founded in 1197 the Monastery of Seedorf, Switzerland. Replica of the shield in the Swiss State Museum, Zürich, in St Vincent's Church, Edinburgh, Scotland. 1 m high, leather and wood.*

423. *Arms of Queen Elizabeth, The Queen Mother. Wall panel, 54 cm in diameter. Wood covered with 3.5-mm leather, carved, painted and gilded.*

424. *The coat of arms of The Old Course Golf and Country Club, St Andrews, Fife, Scotland. 90 × 50 cm. Built up three-dimensionally in pieces of 6.5-mm leather, dyed and gilded; illuminated vellum.*

425. *The Royal Arms of Great Britain and Northern Ireland. Wall panel, 54 cm in diameter, wood carved with 3.5 mm leather, carved, painted and gilded.*

426. *The coat of arms of Sir Charles Ross of Balnagowan. 46 × 30 cm, built up in 3.5 mm leather.*

LOTHAR MÜLLER-WESTPHAL, 1941
(Düren, North Rhineland, West Germany)

With the exception of the coat of arms of the von Drachenfels family (**Fig. 432**), designs in this section are all new creations by the artist.

427. *Bookplate of the artist. Us mingem Böcherschaaf (dialect) means 'from my bookshelf'.*

428. *The coat of arms of the von Eicken family, originating from the Rhineland, now living in Stuttgart, Württemberg, West Germany. 1984.*

429. *The coat of arms of the Fritz family, originating from Bohemia, now living in Grainau, Upper Bavaria, West Germany. 1983.*

430. *Coat of arms of the Schad family in Frankfurt, Hesse, West Germany. 1975.*

431. *Coat of arms of the Frohnapfel family in Fulda, Hesse, West Germany. 1979.*

432. *The ancient coat of arms of the von Drachenfels family, allusive to the name* (Drachen *in German =* 'dragon').

433. *The coat of arms of the Köhler family, originating from Württemberg, now in Bernau, Baden, West Germany. 1972.*

434. *The coat of arms of the Schepper family, originating from Westphalia, now in Herford, Westphalia, West Germany. 1984.*

435. *The coat of arms of the Amend family, originating from Hesse, now in Vallendar near Coblenz, Rhineland, West Germany. 1982.*

436. *The coat of arms of the Ramsauer family, originating from Upper Bavaria, now in Hausham, Upper Bavaria, West Germany. 1984.*

437. *The coat of arms of the Walena family originating from Bohemia, now in Wiesloch, Württemberg, West Germany. 1983.*

438. *The coat of arms of the Köhling family, originating from Westphalia, now in Detmold, Westphalia, West Germany. 1983.*

439. *The coat of arms of the Retzlaff family, originating from East Germany (now Poland), now in Marne, Holstein, West Germany. 1976.*

GUSTAF von NUMERS, 1912–78 (Helsinki, Finland)

von NUMERS

440. *The coat of arms of the von Numers family, Swedish grant from 1653, designed in a revised and modernized style for publication in Skandinavisk Vapenrulla (Scandinavian Roll of Arms) in 1964.*

441. *The coat of arms of the Malm family, the last noble armorial bearings that were granted in Sweden (1974). The family had been raised to nobiliary status in 1810 but without an armorial grant.*

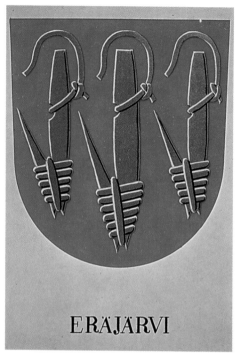

442. *The arms of the rural municipality of Eräjärvi, Finland, designed in 1962. The name of the municipality refers to the hunting men who used these fish-hooks as tackle.*

443. *The arms of the rural municipality of Anttola, Finland, designed in 1962. The municipality is known for its skiers, symbolized here by ancient ski sticks with spear heads.*

444. *These arms have been designed in 1952 for Juho Kusti Paasikivi, President of Finland, 1946–1956, as Knight of the Royal Order of the Seraphim of Sweden (1947) and the Danish Order of the Elephant (1950). The motto is: FOR THE FATHERLAND. The tinctures are azure and argent.*

445. *The coat of arms of Eero Rydman, Lordmayor of Helsinki, 1944–1956, was probably designed for him in 1952 as a Knight of the Danish Order of the Dannebrog (1950). The boat in the banners relates to the arms of the city of Helsinki; the key symbolizes the key of the city.*

447. *The colours of the Carelian Artillery Regiment, designed in 1957.*

446. *The arms of Urho Kaleva Kekkonen, President of Finland, 1956–1981, have been designed for him as a Knight of the Royal Order of the Seraphim of Sweden (1956) and the Danish Order of the Elephant (1957) in 1956. The motto is: HEAR THE SIGHING IN THE SPRUCE.*

448. *Emblem of the Armed Forces of Finland (army, navy and air force), designed in 1963.*

450. *The colours of the Artillery School, designed in 1967.*

449. *The arms of the rural municipality of Pälkäne, Finland, designed in 1965. The cock refers to an ABC-book, of which the wooden cliches were made by the printer Daniel Medelplan (printed in 1719 in Pälkäne).*

451. *The coat of arms of Randall Nybom.*

452. *Exlibris for Christina von Numers, daughter of the artist.*

453. *Exlibris for Gustaf von Numers, the son of the artist.*

454. *Exlibris of Lars Jacob Wrede af Elimä.*

455. *Ragni and Kurt Antell use crest and motto of his arms in their bookplate.*

NORA O'SHEA, 1926 (Herald Painter at the Genealogical Office, Dublin Castle, Ireland)

456. *The arms of Edward MacLysaght, Chief Herald of Ireland, 1943–1954.*

457. *The Office of Arms now The Genealogical Office, Dublin Castle, Ireland, established in 1552.*

458. *The arms of Donal Begley, appointed Chief Herald of Ireland on March 9, 1982.*

459. *The arms of Gerard Slevin, Chief Herald of Ireland, 1955–1981.*

JAN RANEKE, 1914 (Lomma, Sweden)

460. *The coat of arms of Bo Johnson Teutenberg, LL.D., Ambassador at Large and Legal Advisor, Ministry of Foreign Affairs, Stockholm, Sweden.*

461. *The Abrahamsson coat of arms, created in 1982 for Hakan Abrahamsson, Lund, Sweden.*

462. *The Rosensparr arms created for Magnus Rosensparr, Stockholm, Sweden, in 1981.*

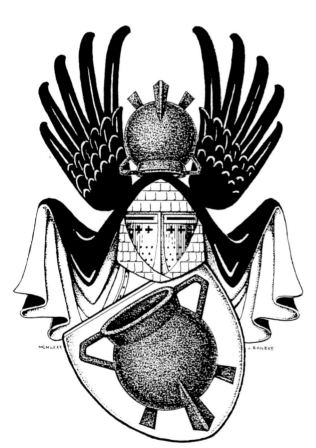

463. *The ancient arms of the Grape family, known since 1325.*

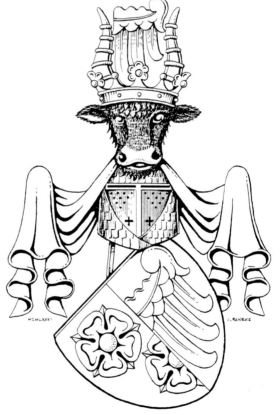

464. *The ancient coat of arms of the von Holstein family, originating from Mecklenburg, Germany.*

197

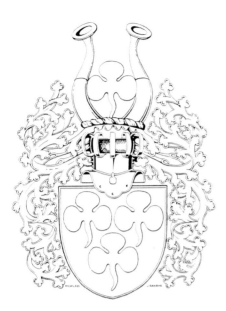

465. *The coat of arms of the Swedish noble family Klöfverskjöld, Stockholm.*

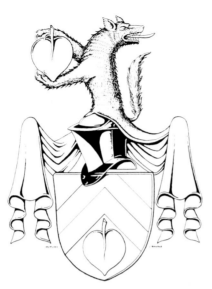

466. *The coat of arms of the Theutenberg family, created in 1979.*

467. *The coat of arms of Torsten Jarnvall, Stockholm, Sweden, created in 1982.*

468. *The coat of arms of Sven and Stig Dingertz, Stockholm, Sweden.*

469. *The coat of arms of Börje Ellerström and his son Nils Erik, Lund, Sweden.*

470. *The coat of arms of Björn Vieweg, Stockholm, Sweden, created in 1983.*

HEINZ RITT, 1918 (Bad Nauheim, Hesse, West Germany)

471. *Vignette designed for posters and programs of the Comedy House Wilhelmsbad in Hanau, Hesse.*

472. *Bookplate of Hans-Enno Korn, Marburg, Hesse, West Germany. In the four corners the arms of the Federal Republic of Germany, the Holy Roman Empire, the city of Marburg and of Hesse.*

Staffel

473. *The arms of Staffel, a township of Limburg an der Lahn, Hesse. Original design by the artist.*

BEARBEITER:
HEINZ F. FRIEDERICHS, HERMANN KNODT✝, HERMANN LING, FRIEDER BOSS, HEINZ RIT.

474. *Design for the 25th anniversary of the* Hessische Wappenrolle *(Hessian Roll of Arms) in 1976, with the arms of the five editor-illustrators combined into one. Published in* Hessische Familienkunde *in 1976.*

❖ Güldener ❖

475. *The coat of arms of the Güldener family, of Bad Nauheim, Hesse, Original design by the artist.*

Frücht

476. *The arms of Frücht, a village in Rhineland-Palatinate. Original design by the artist.*

Ranstadt

477. *The arms of Ranstadt, a village in the County of Friedberg, Hesse. Original design by the artist.*

Figs. 478–485 are German burgher arms which appeared in the series of the *Deutsches Geschlechterbuch*, published by C.A. Starke Verlag, Limburg/Lahn, West Germany.

478. *Schröder, from Verden an der Aller.*

479. *Pollitz, from Lower Saxony.*

480. *Schmidt, from Zella, Willingshausen, Hesse.*

481. *Chelius, from Ober-Widdersheim, Nidda, Hesse.*

482. *Orb, from Pferdersheim, near Worms.*

483. *Tesdorpf, from Ottendorf, Lower Saxony.*

484. *Leyde, from Miswalde, East Prussia.*

485. *Middendorf, from Rechtern, Diepholz.*

Marburg

486. *The arms of the city of Marburg in Hesse, West Germany, published in* Die Hessischen Städtewappen aus Wilhelm Wessels Wappenbuch von 1623, *by Hans-Enno Korn, Kassel, 1984.*

487. *The coat of arms of the Silesian family von Heydebrand und der Lasa, from their history published by C.A. Starke Verlag, Limburg/Lahn, West Germany, 1964.*

488. *The arms of the Hessian capital Wiesbaden with the arms of the Federal Republic of Germany (top), the former Kingdom of Prussia (below), Hesse (left) and Nassau (right), relating to the history of the city. The city arms are azure, three fleurs-de-lis Or (2,1), but there is no historical connection to the arms of the Kings of France.*

MARIA RODRIGUEZ REGUERA, 1917
(León, Spain)

Figs. 489–492 are reproductions of antique wall hangings. All this work is hand-embroidered with antique silk on material (velvet, etc) which is at least a hundred years old.

489. *This design from 1754 was copied from the coat of arms adorning the façade of a palace in Asturias.*

490. *The coat of arms of the family de Vicente.*

491. *The arms of the City of Gijon.*

492. *The civic arms of Aviles (Asturias).*

CARL ROSCHET, 1867–1926 (Basel, Switzerland)

Figs. **493–498** are illustrations from *Wappenbuch der Stadt Basel*, published by Helbing and Lichtenhahn, Basel, 1919–?.

493. *The coat of arms of the Eptingens von Pratteln. In countries of the German language differencing in the shield was never popular, and sometimes different crests were adopted instead. Of the von Eptingen family 52 crests are known.*

494. *The coat of arms of the Eptingens von Blochmont.*

495. *The coat of arms of the ancient noble family of von Altenklingen.*

496. *The coat of arms of the Fröwler family with six additional crests that have served as marks of difference.*

497. *The coat of arms of the von Rotberg family with four additional crests.*

498. *The coat of arms of the Mentelin family.*

P. A. SENCI, 1875–1952 (Trieste, Italy)

Figs. 499–502 are from the *Liber Amicorum* of Dr Ladislao de Lászloczky, Bolzano, Italy.

499. *Arms of Count Enrico del Torso, heraldist in Friuli, Italy, 1875–1955. The chief is the famous capo dell'impero (see also the arms of Nobile Giacomo Carlo Bascapè). 1950.*

500. *The coat of arms of Count Carlo Augusto Bertini Frassoni, Secretary General of the Collegio Araldico, Rome, Italy, 1880–1957. 1950.*

501. *Knight bearing the Polish proclamatio-arms of Pilawa (also the arms of Lászloczky-Lachowski). The bordure of the shield is not part of the arms. 1950.*

502. *The arms of Nobile Giacomo Carlo Bascapè, Milano, Italy, executed in a style inspired by the Rococo. The arms are accompanied by the crosses of the Order of Malta, the Constantinian Order of St George, the Order of the Crown of Italy and the Hungarian Order of Merit.*

JOSÉ RICARDO da SILVA, (Lisbon, Portugal)

Figs. 503–509 are illustrations from *Elucidario Nobiliarchico*, two volumes, 1928–29.

503. *Coat of arms of the Portuguese explorer Fernao de Magalhães (Magellan), c.1480–1521, who circumnavigated the globe. The arms are parted per pale of Magalhães and de Sousa de Arronches.*

504. *Coat of arms of the Portuguese discoverer Vasco da Gama, Count of Vidigueira, c.1469–1524, Admiral of the Indian Ocean, Viceroy of India. The first European to circumnavigate Africa (July, 1497, to August, 1499).*

506. *The coat of arms of the family Franqui de Portugal.*

505. *Coat of arms of Affonso d'Albuquerque, 1453–1515, General-Governor of India (1509–1515) and conqueror of Goa, Malaca, Ormuz, etc.*

507. *The coat of arms of the family de Lacerda.*

508. *The coat of arms of Henry the Navigator, 1394–1460, son of John I, King of Portugal. Through his mother he was a grandson of John of Gaunt, Duke of Lancaster.*

509. *The coat of arms of the family Martins de Deus.*

HUGO GERARD STRÖHL, 1846–1919
(Austrian heraldist)

510. *The arms of the Austro-Hungarian Lands, from* Meyer's Grosses Konversationslexikon, *6th edition, volume 15, Vienna and Leipzig, 1906.*

First row, from left to right: *the Archduchy of Upper Austria, the Archduchy of Lower Austria, the Duchy of Salzburg, the Duchy of Styria, the Duchy of Carinthia, the princely County of Tirol.*

Second row: *the Margraviate of Moravia, the Kingdom of Bohemia, ensigned with the crown of St Wenceslas, the small*

arms of the Austrian Empire. *(The eagle is charged on the breast with the 'genealogical' arms: Habsburg, Austria and Lorrain. The shield is encircled with the collar of the Order of the Golden Fleece.) The small arms of the Kingdom of Hungary, ensigned with the crown of St Stephen, and the Duchy of Carniola.*

Third row: *the Kingdom of Galicia, the Duchy of Silesia, the Duchy of Bukovina, the Kingdom of Croatia, the Margraviate of Istria and the Kingdom of Dalmatia.*

HENK 'tJONG, 1948 (Dordrecht, Netherland)

511. *The arms of the commune Baexem, Limburg, painted for the Hoge Raad van Adel (High Council of the Nobility). St John the Baptist supporting the shield.*

512. *The arms of the polderdistrict De Waterlanden, Noord-Holland, painted for the Hoge Raad van Adel. The coronet is the one for a Dutch marquis, which is often used in Netherland for civic arms. A mermaid (or siren) supports the shield.*

513. *The armorial bearings of the ancient Dutch patrician family Verschoor. Today supporters are not any more the privilege of the titled nobility but may also be used by untitled noblemen and by burghers as well.*

A. TOMADINI (herald painter of the Consulta Araldica del Regno d'Italia, c. 1928–46)

514. *The Duke of Savoy (in the style of the Armorial du héraut Jean Lefèvre). Illustration of 'Stemmi della Real Casa di Savoia', an article in the* Bolletino Ufficiale della Consulta Araldica, *vol. IX, no. 41, May 1931.*

E. PENNETTA (heraldic artist of the Ufficio Araldico presso la Presidenza del Consiglio dei Ministri, Rome, Italy, 1970s)

515. *The arms of the Cassa Risparmio della Provincia di Bolzano (Savings Bank) from the grant by the President of the Republic, 1971.*

KAREL van den SIGTENHORST, 1925
(Rijswijk, Netherland)

WITSIERS

516. *The coat of arms of the Dutch family Witsiers.*

517. *The armorial bearings of Nicol MacInroy of Lude, head of the principal house of the name (Scottish).*

518. *The coat of arms of the von Volborth family (today in Belgium and the USA), personalized for the author by his motto and the cross of a Knight of Justice in the Order of St John (Johanniterorden).*

ANTHONY WOOD, 1925
(Betchworth, Surrey, England)

519. *The armorial bearings of the Scottish Lords Oliphant.*

520. *A broadsheet on Sir John Fordham, Bishop of Durham, embellished with arms and badges of people who played an important part in his life. From left to right: Richard's arms for war, the arms of the See of Ely, where Fordham died of old age, and a fictitious portrait of the bishop; the red rose of Lancaster, the arms of Michael de la Pole and the arms of John of Gaunt. In the centre: the arms of peace of Richard II on his second marriage to Isabella, daughter of Charles VI, King of France, in 1396; the arms of Castile (quartered of Castile and Leon) and the badge of cloud and sunburst of Richard II: in the right corner the planta genista, or broom plant, the badge from which the Plantagenets derived their name. This work was designed, written, gilded and painted between June 1979 and October 1980.*

521. *Detail of the previous illustration. The coat of arms of Sir John Fordham, who was elected Bishop of Durham in 1382. Above the arms of Castile, the badge of cloud and sunburst of Richard II and a planta genista.*

AAGE WULFF, 1918
(Royal Danish herald painter, Copenhagen, Denmark)

522. *The arms of Josephine-Charlotte, Grand Duchess of Luxemburg, as a Lady of the Danish Order of the Elephant, 1976. The Grand Duchess is a daughter of Leopold III, King of the Belgians, and married in 1953 John, Grand Duke of Luxemburg (1964). Her arms are per fess Nassau and Luxemburg impaling Belgium. Fredericksborg Castle, Denmark.*

523. *The coat of arms of Tom Christian Bergroth, Åbo, Finland. The crosses of the crest symbolize his research in the history of orders and medals. Painted in 1980.*

ZDENĚK M. ZENGER, 1913 (Prague, Czechoslovakia)

524. *The arms of the town of Nymburk in Bohemia.*

525. *The coat of arms of the ancient Kings of Bohemia.*

526. *The armorial bearings of Franciscus Cardinal Tomášek, since 1978 Archbishop of Prague, Primate of Bohemia.*

527. *The arms of Jan z Jenštejna, Archbishop of Prague, 1379–1396.*

DESIGN OF NEW ARMORIAL BEARINGS

——— * ———

IN COUNTRIES IN which armorial bearings can be freely assumed (this excludes England, Scotland, Ireland, Spain and South Africa) the following points should be taken into consideration.

1 Make sure that the design is unique and does not infringe upon the rights of others. A coat of arms is personal property, and to have the same or a similar name as an armiger does not mean that one is necessarily related to him and entitled to his arms or a version thereof. If your father's brother, for instance, assumed a coat of arms, this does not mean that you are entitled to use it, unless he made the necessary provisions. If one cannot prove genealogically to descend from an armiger in the male line, he cannot use his arms.

2 Try to keep the design as simple as possible. Arms are still meant to be means of identification and representation and should be easily recognized and remembered. Crowded designs do not answer to this condition.

3 Respect the ethnic background of your family and try to keep the new arms in the style of the country of your origin. If you are, for example, an American citizen, having a German or a French name, don't use the heraldic style and charges which are characteristic for British or Italian heraldry.

4 Do not use badges of Orders of Chivalry as charges for your arms. This can be misleading. Should you be a member of such an order, you can show this outside the actual coat of arms.

5 Do not use coronets, crowns or any other object that may have a particular meaning in the heraldry of the historical noblesse. Do not use supporters, they have a particular significance in heraldry and should not be assumed. Avoid everything that could be interpreted as misleading.

6 In your choice of charges you might search for symbols which express perhaps an occupation or profession that was or is characteristic for members of your family, for a pun on your name (canting arms) or for something relating to the place of origin of your family. There are innumerable possibilities to create a meaningful coat of arms. As for the tinctures you could use your favourite colour combination (preferably limited to one colour and one metal) or the colours of your home town or country.

Charges like the rod of Aesculapius for physicians or the Caduceus for merchants for example have been used only too often and are not very original. Try to avoid heraldic platitudes in a new design. A sailor does not have to use a whole ship. Oars, a sail, a boat or a rudder would do the trick, and artisans could use the tools of their trade, preferably in their medieval form. Show the elements on the shield from the most recognizable angle; a hand seen from the side is meaningless, but palm outwards with space between the fingers is instantly identified.

These are but a few suggestions. At any rate, it is advisable for anybody wanting to assume a coat of arms to consult an experienced and reputable heraldist.

ACKNOWLEDGEMENTS
———— ✳ ————

THROUGHOUT OUR LIFE we learn from what others have thought, found in their research and contributed to the general knowledge of human society, and particularly to our own fields of interest. It is therefore impossible for me to mention all the literature and the authorities that have helped me in my work on the foregoing book. I have consulted libraries, encyclopedias, dictionaries, works on history and on art in general and would like to express my appreciation especially to the authors, illustrators and publishers of the publications I have referred to in the Bibliography.

It also would have been quite impossible to gather all the information if it had not been for several of my colleagues of the International Academy of Heraldry, who aided me in collecting illustration material and/or stood by with their expert advice. Among them I must mention: Cand. phil. Tom Bergroth AIH, curator of the Turku Provincial Museum, Finland; Charles John Burnett AIH, Dingwall pursuivant, head of a department of the National Museum of Antiquities of Scotland; Roger Harmignies AIH, member of the heraldic commission of the Belgian Naval Forces, Hon. Secretary General of the International Confederation of Genealogy and Heraldry; Dr Franz-Heinz von Hye AIH, director of the Municipal Archives of Innsbruck, Austria; Dr Hans-Enno Korn AIH, Councillor of Archives first class at the State Archives of Hesse, West Germany; Dr Ladislao de Lászloczky AIH, Councillor of the Interational Academy of Heraldry, Italy; Faustino Menéndez-Pidal de Navascués, secretary of the Instituto Luis de Salazar y Castro, Spain; Dr Artur de Fraga Norton, Baron de São Roque AIH, adjunct secretary to the Council of the Noblesse and president of its Heraldic Commission, Portugal.

I am also very much indebted to Peter Bander van Duren, publisher in Gerrards Cross, England, the Reverend J. Van Brabant S.J., librarian, University of Antwerp (UFSIA), Belgium, Gerard Crotty, Deputy Chairman of the Heraldry Society of Ireland and Derek Shipley, Knokke-Heist, Belgium. Special thanks go to A. Pallemans, head of a department of the City Library of Antwerp, Belgium, to whom I owe the privilege of being the first to present to the reader colour reproductions of two hitherto unpublished armorial manuscripts: 'Complainte des hérauts d'armes' (fifteenth century) and 'Registre de la confrérie de la Sagrada Passion etc' (1643–1723).

Finally I want to thank all the artists and craftsmen who helped to make this venture more colourful and interesting by enabling me to arrange the international heraldic exhibition in the third part of this book.

Carl-Alexander von Volborth

PHOTOGRAPH CREDITS

Bibliothèque de l'Arsenal, Paris: Figs. 186, 187, 188, 189.

National Library of Scotland, Edinburgh: Figs. 222, 223, 227, 231, 243, 253.

Guy Verwimp, Antwerp: Figs. 170, 171, 180, 181, 182, 183, 184, 185, 232, 233, 237, 238, 240, 241, 245.

Fotostudio Meyer, Antwerp: Figs. 172, 195, 196, 197, 198, 199.

Derk Kinnane Roelofsma, Paris: Figs. 173, 254.

Bildarchiv Foto Marburg, Marburg/Lahn: Figs. 174, 175, 177, 249.

Gerard Crotty, Castle Lyons: Fig. 176.

Margaret Von Hye, Innsbruck: Figs. 178, 179, 190, 191, 194, 206, 275.

Inge Allman, Württemberg: Figs. 192, 200, 201, 203, 207, 226.

Raoul Lagasse, Brussels: Fig. 270.

Carl-Alexander von Volborth: Figs. 193, 204, 205, 234, 235, 242, 244, 255, 265, 266, 273, 274.

Kunsthistorisches Museum, Vienna: Fig. 202.

Victor Bertolaso, Brussels: Fig. 260.

Dieter Prochnow, Ratingen: Figs. 224, 225, 257.

Leo Jouan, OECD: Fig. 267.

DBP (Fröhlich): Figs. 239, 251, 252.

Michel Spiessens, Antwerp: Figs. 236, 258, 259, 261, 263, 268, 269, 271, 272, 347.

Shaw Studios, Brookline: Fig. 325.

Hervé Douxchamps, Brussels: Figs. 276 and 522.

André Snow, Brookline: Figs. 324, 326, 327, 328.

SELECT BIBLIOGRAPHY & RECOMMENDED READING

———— * ————

HISTORY OF ART

Helen Gardner, *Art Through the Ages*, New York 1980.
E.H. Gombrich, *The Story of Art*, London 1983.

HERALDIC DESIGN

Heather Child, *Heraldic Design, A Handbook for Students*, London 1979.
W.H. St. John Hope, *Heraldry for Craftsmen and Designers*, London 1913.
Ad. Matthias Hildebrandt, *Heraldisches Musterbuch*, Neustadt a.d Aisch 1975.
Heinrich Hussman, *Über Deutsche Wappenkunst*, Wiesbaden 1973.
J.C.P.W.A. Steenkamp, *Heraldiek In Kunsthistorischen En Aesthetischen Zin*, Amsterdam 1948.
Carl-Alexander von Volborth, *Het Wapen, Stijl En Vorm*, Handzame 1971. German and French enlarged editions: *Das Wappen, Stil Und Form*, Limburg an der Lahn 1977. *L'Art Héraldique, Styles Et Formes*, Brussels 1982.

HERALDIC TEXTBOOKS

F.P. de Almeida Langhans, *Heráldica, Ciência De Temas Vivos*, Lisbon 1966.
Arvid Bergman, *Heraldisk Bilderbok*, Stockholm 1951.
J.P. Brooke-Little, *Boutell's Heraldry*, London and New York 1978.
J.A. De Boo, *Heraldiek*, Bussum 1973.
Charles Norton Elvin, *A Dictionary of Heraldry*, London 1969.
Arthur Charles Fox-Davies, *A Complete Guide to Heraldry*, New York 1978.

Julian Franklyn *Shield and Crest*, London 1960.
D.L. Galbreath and Léon Jéquier, *Manuel du Blason*, Lausanne 1977.
Marian Gumowski, *Handbuch der Polnischen Heraldik*, Graz 1969.
Bruno Bernard Heim, *Heraldry In The Catholic Church, Its Origin, Customs And Laws*, Gerrards Cross 1978.
Ad. Matthias Hildebrandt, *Wappenfibel, Handbuch Der Heraldik*, revised and enlarged by the Heralds-Commission of the 'Deutsche Wappenrolle', Neustadt a.d. Aisch 1967.
Sir Thomas Innes of Learney, *Scots Heraldry*, Edinburgh, 1956.
Pierre Joubert, *Les Lys Et Les Lions*, Paris 1942.
Rémi Mathieu, *Le Système Héraldique Français*, Paris 1946.
Iain Moncreiffe and Don Pottinger, *Simple Heraldry Cheerfully Illustrated*, London 1953.
Ottfried Neubecker, *Heraldry: Sources, Symbols And Meaning*, Maidenhead 1976. Also available in French and German.
C. Pama, *Rietstap's Handboek Der Wapenkunde* Leiden 1961.
Hugo Gerard Ströhl, *Heraldischer Atlas*, Stuttgart 1899.
Carl-Alexander von Volborth, *Alverdens Heraldik I Farver*, Copenhagen 1972. English and German editions: *Heraldry Of The World*, London 1973: New York 1974; *Heraldik Aus Aller Welt In Farben*, Berlin 1973. *Heraldry: Customs, Rules And Styles*, Poole, Dorset 1981. *Heraldiek*, Amsterdam/Dieren, 1985.
F. Warnecke, *Heraldisches Handbuch*, reprint Limburg/Lahn 1971.
John Woodward and George Burnett, *Woodward's A Treatise On Heraldry*, reprinted in 1969.

INDEX OF NAMES

✳

General Index